2 CORINTHIANS

GEOFFREY GROGAN

CHRISTIAN FOCUS PUBLICATIONS

© 1996 Geoffrey W. Grogan
ISBN 1-85792-220-4

Published by
Christian Focus Publications Ltd
Geanies House, Fearn, Ross-shire,
IV20 1TW, Scotland, Great Britain.

Cover design by Donna Macleod

Printed and bound in Great Britain by
The Guernsey Press Co. Ltd., Guernsey, Channel Islands

Contents

For Eva,
whose loving and prayerful support is an
immense encouragement to me in all my work.

Special thanks to Elizabeth Lockhart,
a Christian friend of the family, who has read this and
my other two most recent books in manuscript to see
if they are written in good plain English rather than
in incomprehensible theological jargon.
She has made some helpful suggestions for improve-
ment, but if anything still makes no sense,
I am the person to blame!

HOW TO USE THIS BOOK

This book is a commentary, an attempt to interpret the teaching of a book of the Bible. It is, however, a commentary with a difference. It has been a purpose of the writer to make it useful as a means of preparation for Christian service. This feature is not for the select few, for all Christians are called to serve God.

At the close of each chapter except the first, you will find a series of questions. If you want to gain maximum profit from the book, you will use these as means of self-interrogation, to show you whether you have really been learning lessons in Christian service, the kind of lessons that this Bible book is particularly fitted to teach.

Every commentary on a Bible book should be used as an aid to the study of the text of that Bible book itself, not as a substitute for it. This is not just because every student of literature should have plenty of direct contact with the text, but especially because this is the Word of God and it is important to hear God's Word for yourself. In this regard, the present book is no exception.

You would find it advisable to read Second Corinthians in the New International Version or some other modern translation. Every version has its strengths and weaknesses, but the Authorised Version, though incomparable from a literary point of view and of high spiritual quality, is perhaps at its weakest in its translation of Second Corinthians.

I suggest you adopt the following plan:
1. Read Chapter 1, which introduces Second Corinthians.
2. Read the section of 2 Corinthians with which Chapter 2 deals.

3. Read Chapter 2 itself.

4. Think prayerfully about the questions. Try to be honest.

5. Proceed through the book by the same method as in 2-4 above.

6. Read Chapter 1 again.

INTRODUCTION TO THE LETTER

No New Testament letter is more needed by the church today than Paul's Second Epistle to the Corinthians.

Does it scratch where the modern church itches? Not necessarily, for a church is not always conscious of its need. What it does rather is to bring a surgeon's knife to the place where a cancer is developing, often all unseen.

This is true of both of Paul's letters to the Corinthians, but there is something particularly distinctive about the Second. It has much to say about Christian service, and presents a picture of a Christian leader very much at variance with the image of leadership current in many church circles today. The image of Christian service a church has is bound to be deeply affected by the kind of leaders it has. For that reason too we all need exposure to this letter.

Its message cuts very deeply. To study it and apply its teaching can be very uncomfortable, but if the contemporary church is to be true to its Lord, this cries out to be done.

This does not mean there is no message of comfort or of encouragement here, for there certainly is, but it does mean that the healing balm will only come to those prepared to accept the cuts made by that operating knife.

Perhaps all we have said so far simply means that this is the Word of God and not simply of a man, for God never speaks superficially but always radically – if we have ears to hear.

1. Paul the church-planter

This is a letter from a church-planter to a local fellowship of Christians, whose founder members owe their salvation, under God, to his work.

What sort of person is a church-planter? Not simply an evangelist, but someone with a variety of gifts – evangelistic, theological, pastoral and organizational.

There must be a clear understanding of the gospel and a God-imparted gift for communicating it. Also it is important to be able to identify central truth and teach it clearly and relevantly. There must certainly be a love for people and a concern to get them started on the basics of Christian discipleship. Some organizational skill too is needed, not simply the kind gained through management or business studies, but what comes from understanding the Bible teaching about the local church and the principles on which its life is to be structured.

If anybody had this range of gifts in full measure it was the apostle Paul, and, under God, he was responsible for planting many of the earliest churches in what are now Greece and western Turkey.

Unknown to him at the time, his preparation for this work started before he became a Christian. He gained considerable knowledge of the Old Testament.

As a Pharisee, he would be concerned about the human organization of synagogues, and local Christian churches were largely patterned on the synagogues. He may too have had a concern to gain proselytes (Gentile converts) to Judaism.

All this, however, would have been valueless apart from the dynamic experience in which Christ both claimed and commissioned him. This made him a Christ-centred man, with a passion to bring people to the Saviour and to build them into local fellowships which could in turn become evangelistic centres.

This evangelistic passion was exercised on his three missionary journeys, each commencing from Antioch (Acts 13:1-4; 15:30-41; 18:23), the second major evangelistic base of the Christian church (Jerusalem was the first).

During these journeys we see him working with other evangelists like Barnabas, Mark, Silas and Timothy.

They usually started in synagogues. This was because it was the Jews who had received the Old Testament promises about a coming Christ, and so it was only right they should be the first to hear of his actual coming. There they would also find proselytes (formal Gentile converts to Judaism) and 'God-fearers' (interested Gentile enquirers), many of whom would have good knowledge of the Old Testament, which, in theory at least, should have conditioned them to an intelligent hearing of the gospel.

Churches were planted, and Paul was eager, not only to take the gospel further, but also to nurture these infant fellowships. They needed to know how the Old Testament Scriptures witnessed to Christ, to see the theological and ethical implications of the gospel, and to learn what attitudes Christians should have.

2. How the good news came to Corinth

Luke tells us (Acts 18:1-18) that Paul founded the church there during his Second Missionary Journey.

a. *The city of Corinth*

Corinth was a fairly new city in Paul's day. Destroyed by the Romans in 146 BC, it had been rebuilt and resettled in 44 BC. In 27 BC the Romans made it the capital of their new province of Achaia. Magnificent public buildings were now erected.

Even the old Corinth had a reputation for wealth, but the new Corinthians had a passion to achieve riches, for their city was settled largely by freedmen, slaves whose services to their masters had earned them their freedom. These were often gifted and were notoriously ambitious for wealth and status. They were *nouveaux riches*, self-made men, and they loved self-display.

Corinth was well placed for trade, straddling an isthmus which had the one land route into southern Greece, and which was narrow enough to transport goods across it. This saved merchants from risking the dangerous sea journey round the southern coast.

Many merchants came from other lands, especially from the east, and settled in Corinth. This meant that its manufactured products, particularly in metal and pottery, were sent far and wide. People also converged on it for the biennial Isthmian games, second in prestige only to the Olympics, and this was another important economic factor. There was also plenty of good agricultural land in its hinterland.

As in all Greek cities, the intellectual elite were influenced by various philosophies, but it was the religious cults that were really popular. Corinth had many of them, and the temples of Aphrodite and of Poseidon were particularly important. In earlier days, according to Strabo, the shrine of Aphrodite had a thousand prostitutes. Corinthians still had an unsavoury sexual reputation, not helped by the fact that their city was a major seaport. Paul was in Corinth when he wrote Romans 1:18-32, with its indictment of Gentile sin, probably reflecting what he saw there.

Although Greek, Corinth had something of a Roman atmosphere. Nero loved it, and he spent time in it, receiving great adulation there. He well symbolized the typical image of greatness the Corinthians had in their minds.

b. *Paul's first visit to Corinth*

Paul stayed there at least one and a half years (Acts 18:11,18). He lived with Aquila and Priscilla, who were not only fellow-Jews (although some have suggested Priscilla may have been a Roman aristocrat), but fellow tent-makers. The seamen of Corinth used small tents as protection from the elements.

Many Corinthians were converted, but Paul faced antagonism from the Jews, although the synagogue ruler, Crispus, became a Christian. The reference Luke makes to Gallio (Acts

18:12-17) is helpful historically, for he was proconsul of Corinth for just one year, and we know which year: it was AD 51-52.

c. *His concern for a strong church there*
Every historian has to be selective, for he cannot record everything. In the Acts of the Apostles, Luke tells the story of the early church. It is clear from his selection of events, confirmed at times from other parts of the New Testament, that certain churches were established as major evangelistic centres. From these the gospel could move out. This was certainly true of Jerusalem, Antioch and Ephesus.

It was urgent that the good news of Jesus should be proclaimed widely, but the apostolic preachers and teachers did not themselves go to every village and settlement. Instead they spent time in major centres. This was to secure strong churches as bases for evangelistic outreach into their areas of influence.

The strategic nature of Corinth for evangelistic outreach was plain to see. It was a large and busy commercial centre, visited not only by other Greeks but by many foreigners. It was the gateway to southern Greece, and a seaport which harboured from time to time ships from many different parts of the Mediterranean world.

3. Problems, problems, problems!

a. *What the church at Corinth was like*
1 Corinthians 1:26-29 should be noted but not over-emphasized. Without doubt there were some higher class people in the church, probably in leadership positions. There was a synagogue ruler (Acts 18:8; 1 Cor. 1:14), and Erastus (mentioned in Romans 16:23, written from Corinth) was a major city official. Other people like Chloe, Gaius and Stephanus (1 Cor. 1:11,14,16) may have been quite well-to-do. There were both Jews and Gentiles there.

The church may have been fairly large, and so would meet in several homes, perhaps fostering a competitive party-spirit. Have modern Christians never said, 'Our house-group is bigger than yours'?

The Corinthian epistles are of great value because they show us what an early Christian community was like. This church was clearly an exciting place to be, with lively worship and fascinating personalities. The city of Corinth had many similarities to cities in the West today, so that the church there was subject to some of the pressures and many of the problems we face today in our own church life.

If we knew nothing of the city of Corinth we could almost deduce many of its characteristics from 1 Corinthians, for the weaknesses of a church are so often reflections of the society in which it is located.

We see this culture's competitiveness in the church's party spirit, its intellectualism in the quest for wisdom and knowledge, its licentiousness in the problems of sexual morality, its paganism in the questions related to idolatry, its desire for display in the exaltation of the more showy spiritual gifts, and its emphasis on incorporeal immortality in the debate about the resurrection.

What about Second Corinthians? It might appear that the issues here are completely different, but this is not altogether true.

The problems in 1 Corinthians sprang largely from the values they had imbibed from their environment. Their criticisms of Paul, which made it necessary for him to write a letter like 2 Corinthians, were influenced by their image of what a leader should be, and this too reflected their environment. Leadership style and the principles of Christian ministry constitute the great theme of this second letter.

Of course, Paul's contacts with the Corinthian church were

not all by letter. Not only did he visit it several times himself, but he also sent both Timothy (1 Cor. 4:17) and Titus (2 Cor. 7:6,7), as well as at least two other men whose names we do not know (2 Cor. 8:16-24), to minister in various ways to the church there. Not only so, but he had a letter from them, and also there were visits from two groups of members known to us (1 Cor. 1:11, 16; 16:15-18).

b. *Paul's opponents there*

Who were his opponents at Corinth? What kind of people were they? It is not easy to tell, as there is too little express information in the letter.

If there was only one group, they were certainly Jews (11:22). T.B. Savage, drawing his picture of them from chapters 10 to 13, says, 'All we really know is that they were Jewish (2 Cor. 11:22) and outsiders (11:4). Beyond that we may infer that they preached a different Jesus from Paul (11:4), were intruding into his sphere of ministry (10:12-18), were receiving financial support (11:12) and were behaving in a heavy-handed manner (11:18-20).' [1]

There are two main views among the welter of theories.

Were they Judaizing Christians from Palestine, very much like the Galatian heretics who insisted that circumcision must be added to simple faith for Gentile converts? This theory is based largely on 11:4.

Or was their outlook more Hellenistic? For example, did they think of the future life as being without bodily form, so prompting Paul to write not only 1 Corinthians 15 but also 2 Corinthians 5?

Probably we would be best to follow scholars like C.K. Barrett and T. B. Savage who hold that the incomers were Judaiz-

---

1. Timothy B. Savage, *Power through Weakness: Paul's understanding of the Christian ministry in 2 Corinthians*, Cambridge, CUP, 1996, p. 10.

ers but that they formed an alliance with disaffected Hellenistic Jewish Christians at Corinth, whose outlook had posed problems for Paul earlier, problems reflected in 1 Corinthians. We recall that the Pharisees and Herodians, whose outlooks were diametrically opposed, united with each other in opposition to Jesus (Mark 3:6), and the same sort of thing may well have happened in Corinth.

The incomers seem to have arrived on the scene at a later stage in the growth of the church than they did at Galatia, where they probably came quite early and so disrupted the church at a formative stage.

c. *Paul's dealings with the church*

It is not easy to sort out the course of these. See 'The Chronology of Paul's Contacts with the Church at Corinth' which follows this Introduction.

He seems to have kept in close touch with the way things were moving in the church there, by personal visits, by visits from members of his team, and by letters, two of which we possess while others are not extant.

What comes through so strongly is the consistently pastoral motivation of all his contacts with them. This is true even where he is dealing with the criticism that on one occasion he had not come to them as promised (1:23-2:4).

For Paul there could be no question of preaching the gospel in an area, establishing a church there and then going away to other areas and forgetting all about it. He had a passion for a church's faithfulness to Christ, for its growth, for its maturing. Those he had led to Christ were constantly in his heart and in his prayers.

4. Giving not the gospel only but himself also

a. *The revelation of the personality and character of Paul*
From Paul's Corinthian correspondence and particularly from
the Second Epistle we gain some valuable insights into the personality and character of the man himself. A study of Second
Corinthians would certainly undermine some of the images
many people have of him.

How does he come across?

We see him as a most able teacher, well able to relate Christian teaching to the practical situations faced in the churches.

We also see him as a most diligent, responsible and sensitive
pastor. He knew when to be gentle and tender, and when to be
strong and stern. He writes very courteously, and when he moves
into irony that sometimes has a sharp edge to it, this is only
because the necessities of the situation made it unavoidable.

We see too that he was a sensitive man, and that he could be
hurt. Yet this did not make him retreat into his shell, or lead to
sulking, but rather to a warm appeal to his readers to open their
hearts to him and to consider the arguments he was able to make
in his defence.

Was he over-defensive? Some have thought so.

We can only really assess this, however, when we realise
what issues were at stake. Without doubt they were major ones.
The criticisms of him, if true and appropriate, would have un-
dermined his whole ministry, and might even have led eventually to a complete breakdown of assurance of salvation for the
Corinthian Christians themselves. 'Could God really have
worked through such a man to bring us to Christ?', they might
have asked themselves, and then gone on to ask, 'Are we then
really Christians at all?'

b. *What the letters teach us about Paul as a Christian worker*

Because Paul's letter to them was so self-revelatory, it shows us very clearly the principles of his Christian service. These are basic principles which have very wide application in every age and place. No two churches are ever the same, so that exact parallels between pastoral situations today and those in the Corinthian church may be rare, but Paul's principles of operation were so fundamental, and so related to the gospel itself, that they must be of abiding and permanent validity.

They present a conception of a Christian worker very different from that held by many of the Corinthians, and, it must be said, in many of our churches today.

Mass means of communication have provided many new avenues for the proclamation of the gospel, but there is no doubt that our image of an effective Christian worker may be influenced by them. We can think that what matters most is appearance, eloquence, communication skills, and, for leadership in churches, also business and management skills.

None of these is without its value, but they are not in the same league as the spiritual qualities we see here in Paul, such as faithfulness to the gospel, sensitivity to people, the humility of Christ, acceptance of the cross and willingness to be persecuted and reviled for Christ's sake. These are not imparted by courses but by the sanctifying work of the Holy Spirit who seeks to mould us into Christlike people.

5. What sort of letter?

a. *The integrity of the letter*

At various times, it has been suggested that Second Corinthians, as we have it, is not a unity. Most who have made this point have accepted that all the chapters were written by Paul and all of them to the Corinthians, but not at the same time. Various scholars have made this suggestion about different parts of the letter, about 2:14 to 7:4, about a smaller section of this, namely 6:14 to 7:1, about chapters 8 and 9 and about chapters 10 to 13.

The two most persistent of these views have been those associated with 6:14 to 7:1 and chapters 10 to 13, and these need to be taken seriously, although the present writer is convinced of the literary unity of the letter.

Murray Harris expresses well the main argument against *chapters 10 to 13* being part of the same letter as chapters 1 to 9 when he refers to 'the change of tone at 2 Corinthians 10:1, which is announced, unexpected, pronounced and sustained...'[2] It is interesting though that, despite this, his commentary tentatively assumes the letter's unity.

An important point, often missed, relates to the way Paul praises and blames his readers in his epistles generally. If he wants to praise a church but also needs to criticize it, he always starts with the commendations. An examination of Romans, 1 and 2 Thessalonians and even Philippians (with its late reference to Euodia and Syntyche) shows us this. The risen Lord follows exactly the same course in the Letters to the Seven Churches in Revelation 2 and 3.

Viewed in this light, the change from chapters 1 to 9 to chapters 10 to 13 is simply the major example of a general phenomenon. It could well be that it was a part and not the whole of the church that was taken in by the false teachers who had come into the church and their strong criticisms of Paul, and so needed the last four chapters, but it was safe to send them to the whole church as part of this epistle. A note to this effect would have helped us, as modern readers, but the recipients would see for whom they were chiefly intended.

What is the real tone of 10-13? How severe is it? O'Connor

---

2. Murray J. Harris, '2 Corinthians' in F.E. Gaebelein (ed.), *Expositor's Bible Commentary,* Vol. 10, Grand Rapids, Zondervan, 1976, p. 304.

refers to 'the savage reproaches and sarcastic self-vindication of chapters 10-13'.[3] Is this really fair comment? It squares ill with the tender beginning (10:1), with his affirmations of his love for his readers in 12:14, 15, with the warmth of the word 'brothers' in 13:11 and with the tone of the last four verses of his letter. It is worth remembering too that Jewish wit was and in fact still is strongly ironic, so that it would be seen to be appropriate when directed against opponents who were themselves Jewish.

We can characterize these chapters as strong but pastoral, but we should remember that pastoral letters are written by spiritual shepherds and that these recognise the existence not only of erring sheep but also of wolves. In chapters 10-13 Paul is still writing to sheep, but he refers to wolves, and especially in 11:3-15.

What about *6:14-7:1*? Certainly it seems somewhat intrusive. We will note a little later, however, that digression is one of the features of Paul's style, and this passage may well be an example of this, a digression probably sparked off by the phrase, 'I speak as to my children' in 6:13. Paul's loving concern for his Corinthian 'family' leads him to warn them against compromise, and the loving motive of this is revealed again in the words 'dear friends' in the last verse of this section, as well as the heartfelt sentiments of 7:2-4.

If Second Corinthians has given some readers the impression that it is a kind of 'scissors and paste' composition, we should remember that Paul was writing in a situation of serious controversy. His style here perhaps reveals a certain agitation of spirit in the writer. Galatians too is like that, and nobody has seriously suggested it is not a unity.

In considering the integrity of any piece of literature that

---

3. J. Murphy-O'Connor, *The Theology of the Second Letter to the Corinthians*, Cambridge, C.U.P., 1991, p. 12.

has come down to us as a unity, we should treat is as such if it makes good sense. This does not mean there will be no difficulties in doing this. After all, there are sometimes similar difficulties with literature whose integrity has never been doubted.

b. *Its relationship to 1 Corinthians*

First Corinthians was written to deal with problems in the church, many of them outlined in a letter he had received from it. Some of these were theological, while others were ethical and pastoral. Second Corinthians too is a problem-addressing letter, but in many ways it is quite different, for, rather than handling different issues one by one, this letter instead seeks to deal with the whole spiritual ethos of the church as shown in its view as to the marks of a true servant of Christ.

In terms of their spiritual message, the relationship between the two letters is most instructive and challenging. It is clear from the first letter that there was a lot of spiritual pride in the Corinthian church, pride of party, pride of wisdom, pride of freedom, pride of gift, pride of theology. Paul deals with these issues piece-meal, but does he deal adequately with the spiritual disposition that unites them all? It would not seem so, but in fact he goes on to do this in his Second Letter.

The real problem with spiritual pride is that it is an utter denial of the principle of the cross, which is at the heart both of the gospel and of the authentic Christian lifestyle. This is the principle of all Christian service as both taught and demonstrated in this epistle and its writer, and never more so than in its last four chapters.

Who would be so bold as to say that the modern church does not need this teaching?

c. *Literary features of the letter*

As a literary product it has a number of very interesting features.

Readers of Paul's letters are familiar with *his tendency to go off at a tangent*. He leaves his main argument for a while to discuss some theme, usually an exalted one, before rejoining the main line of argument once more. This usually happens where some phrase he has employed is used by the Holy Spirit to stimulate great thoughts. There are examples of this kind of thing, for instance, in Ephesians, where 3:14-21 is probably the conclusion to a prayer he began in 1:15-19a and where 3:2-13 appears to be another digression. The great 'hymn to Christ' in Philippians 2:6-11 may be another example.

There are at least two digressions of this sort in Second Corinthians. We have already noted and commented on 6:14-7:1. The longest of such digressions is, however, the one that extends from 2 Corinthians 2:14 to 7:4, and, of course, it includes the smaller digression to which we have already referred. This long passage is known to scholars as 'the Great Digression'. The accusations some at Corinth have made against Paul touch very sensitively his concept of what Christian service really is, and so, thus stimulated, he writes these great chapters.

One characteristic of this epistle is *the way the apostle writes at times in a terse, staccato fashion*, often with the constant repetition of a key word or phrase.

In 11:26, for example, he writes eight consecutive two or three word phrases, each commencing with *kindunois* ('in danger'). In 6:4-7, this feature is even more extensive, for there are no less than eighteen brief phrases each commencing with the Greek *en* 'in'. These are simply two of the more striking examples, but there are plenty more, such as his repeated 'but not' in 4:8, 9, and the repetition of 'So am I' in 11:22. There are plenty of rhetorical questions, sometimes in sequence, as in passages like 6:14-16 and 11:29.

Because many of these passages are autobiographical, they are highly suggestive, and make us turn to the Acts of the Apostles in search of illustrations of them.

Paul *had a gift of illustration*. His illustrations are rarely expounded at length (the 'body' in 1 Corinthians 12 is one exception to this), and there is little in his writings to correspond to the parables of our Lord.

Sometimes in fact they consist simply of picturesque words or phrases, which set the Christian imagination to work. What thoughts can be evoked by a phrase like 'Christ, who is the image of God' in 4:4 or 'a new creation', applied to the Christian in 5:17? Whole books might be written in exposition of these two vivid illustrations, both of course based on Genesis 1.

In the commentary we note *a number of places where a word or phrase may be translated or interpreted in two ways*. See, for example, the comments on 3:18 and 4:6 and 7. Often there is a great deal to be said for both, and this raises the possibility that the ambiguity is deliberate, and that Paul uses language with two possible meanings because both are true.

The epistle contains theological material, where Paul is expounding some great Christian theme, like the glory of the gospel of Christ (chapters 3 and 4) or reconciliation through Christ (chapter 5), but there are also strongly pastoral passages, where his concern for the church is strongly felt, such as chapters 8 and 9, 12 and 13.

What is particularly marked in this letter, however, is *the personal and sometimes autobiographical note*, and this is interwoven with the theological and the pastoral. There is in fact no chapter written simply in theological treatise form, but everything is touched by the personal. Preaching has been called, 'truth through personality'. It is not a fully adequate definition, but what is true in it could be amply illustrated from this letter, in which Paul is very much the preacher as well as the pastor.

d. *Its major theme*

If this personal note gives unity to the book, so also does the one subject which keeps making its appearance, and which is never really completely out of sight. This is the theme of the nature of Christian service. In fact, this letter is really Paul's *magnum opus* on the theme, and this is made all the more valuable by the personal touches that keep appearing.

In 1 Corinthians, chapters 1 to 4, Paul expounds Divine wisdom in such a way as to show how it cuts right across human wisdom. Throughout Second Corinthians he does the same kind of thing in relation to Christian service. The Christian preacher is no mere variant of the Greek rhetorician any more than the Christian leader is of a modern business executive.

There are in fact deep spiritual principles at the heart of true Christian service and these arise from the gospel itself, which finds its centre in the greatest of all acts of service to God, performed by a Man when he hung in agony upon a cross. True Christian service is therefore humble, costly and sacrificial.

In a sense, this supplies the key to the irony which is such a feature of the letter and especially of chapters 10 to 13. The Kingdom of God, taught by and incarnated by Christ, has been called 'The upside-down kingdom' for its values cut right across those which worldly kingdoms so often espouse.

So we find Paul 'boasting' about his weaknesses (11:30; 12:9), and asking forgiveness for his failure to lord it in arrogant fashion over the Corinthians (11:18-21)!

This literary irony is really an extension of the dramatic irony found in the records of the passion and death of Christ, where thorns do service for a crown, and a rough tree and nails for a throne, with sarcastic cries of bitter hatred for shouts of triumphant recognition of a King.

If you are not keen to have your own practice of Christian service and your motives for doing it disturbed, you had better avoid Second Corinthians!

CHRONOLOGY OF PAUL'S CONTACTS WITH THE CHURCH AT CORINTH

50-51 PAUL'S 1st VISIT – Church planted –1½ years	Acts 18:1-11
52-54 **'The Previous letter'**	*1*:5:9,10
Visit or letter to Paul from house of Chloe	*1*:1:11
Visit to Paul from Stephanus, etc.	*1*:16:17
Letter from church to Paul asking for advice	*1*:7:1
55 **1 Corinthians from Ephesus**	*1*:16:8
Titus to Corinth probably taking 1 Corinthians	*2*:8:6
Titus returns to Paul (presumably)	
Timothy to Corinth	*1*:4:17; 16:10
Timothy returns to Paul	*1*:16:11
PAUL'S 2nd VISIT - 'the Painful Visit'	*1*:4:19; 16:5; *2*:2:1
56 **'The Painful Letter'**- taken by Titus	*2*:2:3,4; 7:6-8
Titus returns to Paul	*2*:2:13; 7:5-7
56-57 **2 Corinthians from Macedonia**	*2*:9:1-4
PAUL'S 3rd VISIT – 3 months	*2*:9:5; 12:14; 13:1,2; Acts 20:2,3.

N.B.   a. *1* = 1 Corinthians. *2* = 2 Corinthians
       b. This chronology assumes the integrity of 2 Corinthians.
       c. Some of the dates may vary by one year.

Some suggested books for further reading

C.K. Barrett, *A Commentary on the Second Epistle to the Corinthians*, New York: Harper, 1973

E. Best, *Second Corinthians*, Louisville, John Knox Press, 1987

Roy Clements, *The Strength of Weakness*, Tain: Christian Focus Publications, 1994 [1]

F.W. Danker, *2 Corinthians*, Minneapolis; Augsburg Press, 1989

James Denney, *The Second Epistle to the Corinthians*, London: Hodder and Stoughton, 1894

G.W. Grogan *Wrestling with the Big Issues*, Tain: Christian Focus Publications, 1993 [2]

M.J. Harris, '2 Corinthians' in FE Gaebelein (ed.), *Expositor's Bible Commentary*. Grand Rapids: Zondervan, Vol. 10, 1976, pp. 301-406.

P.E. Hughes, *Paul's Second Epistle to the Corinthians*, Grand Rapids: Eerdmans, 1962

R.P. Martin, *2 Corinthians*, Waco: Word, 1986
                    1 and 2 Corinthians, Word Biblical Themes, Word, 1988

R.V.G. Tasker, *2 Corinthians: an Introduction and Commentary* (Tyndale New Testament Commentaries), Leicester, IVP, 1958

---

1. A series of sermons on Second Corinthians.
2. Shows how Paul dealt with problems.

1: STRENGTHENED AND STRENGTHENING OTHERS (1:1-11)

1. His greetings (1:1,2)

When I write to a fellow-Christian, I usually end my letter with the words, 'with warmest Christian greetings'. Many Christians do something similar. From whom did we learn this? Probably from each other but there can be little doubt that this kind of greeting came ultimately from the New Testament writers, whose salutations always have a strongly Christian tone.

In the New Testament letters however the greetings normally come at the beginning, although you sometimes find them at the end as well, as a glance at 1 Corinthians 16:21-24 or Philippians 4:21-23 will soon show.

This makes us aware of the fact that the Christian faith, which, in Paul's day, was such a new phenomenon, transformed everything it touched, as it still does. This applied even to such a thing as the forms of greeting people used in their letters. Here, as in the introductions to most of his other letters too, Paul was taking traditional forms of greeting and adapting them in different ways, putting them to the service of Christ's gospel. There is, in fact, much we can use in the service of the gospel, provided that service transmits the gospel's authentic content and does not cloud or alter it.

First of all, he does a completely normal thing. He gives his name and makes reference to those to whom he is writing.

Then however he modifies the word of greeting that was standard in Greek letters. This was *chara*, meaning 'joy'. Why does he alter this? Is there no joy in the Christian life? Of course there is and Paul himself asserts this very plainly in Galatians 5:22, when he says, 'The fruit of the Spirit is ... joy.' In fact he refers very soon to 'your joy' (1:24) and then to 'my joy' (2:3).

Joy is not however as fundamental to the Christian life as

grace. Paul was a very clear Christian thinker, and he was never in danger of confusing roots and fruit. Grace is the root, and joy a fruit of what God has done in bringing us to himself. So he changes *chara* to the similar-sounding *charis*, 'grace'.

Grace is simply 'unmerited favour', and it is the basis of everything the Christian enjoys in Christ. It is for Christ's sake we are accepted by God and there is nothing we have done, or are doing, or even promise or hope to do which can be a substitute for this. Acceptance with God is to be received by faith, not earned by works we mistakenly think to be meritorious.

He follows 'grace' with a very rich word, the normal term employed by Jews when they greeted each other. This would remind the readers of the roots of their faith, which were in the Hebrew Scriptures.

This word *eirene*, usually rendered 'peace', is actually so full of meaning as to be almost untranslatable, although 'well-being' would not be too wide of the mark. It sums up the very practical difference Christ and the salvation God has given us through him have made to us. We are no longer outsiders; we have been welcomed into a place of peace, love, security, warmth, fellowship and plenty, a place of sure and certain hope.

In the whole of chapter 1, verses 1 to 11, as in so much he says later in his letter, Paul constantly reminds his readers of the Source of all the blessings Christians receive. That Source is 'God' (v.9) or 'the God and Father of our Lord Jesus Christ' (v.3) or 'Christ' (v.5). In verse 2, he articulates this as 'God our Father and the Lord Jesus Christ'.

We need to ponder these words and take seriously what they reveal about Paul's view of Christ. Clearly he saw him as an equal Source of Divine blessing, equal, that is, with God himself. This is quite staggering. Who is he writing about? A Man who died at thirty-three on a Roman scaffold! Remember too that Paul, as a Jew, was a monotheist through and through.

Could we have misunderstood him? Is he simply indulging in a kind of literary short-cut, so that all he really means is that grace comes from God and peace from Christ? Even if this were to be his meaning, its implications would be colossal, given the fulness of meaning we have already seen attaches to the word *eirene*.

This can hardly be his intended meaning, however, for in the ending of this letter, he ascribes grace specifically to Christ in the famous words, 'May the grace of the Lord Jesus Christ ... be with you all' (13:14). It is quite clear that he viewed his Lord as fully divine. To him the Jesus of Nazareth who had lived and taught and suffered and died and risen from the dead was as truly God as God the Father. There is just no way in which the great significance of the words he has written here can be reduced.

There may even be significance in the fact that here he uses the word 'our' of the Father but not of the Lord Jesus Christ. Because the Father is God he may seem remote, but this possessive pronoun adds a note of intimacy. On the other hand, because Jesus is truly human, we may be tempted to forget his divine majesty. God is not just the Father, but *our* Father; Jesus is not just our Lord but *the* Lord.

What kind of status did Paul's letter have for those who first read it? It came to them with divine authority, for Paul's reference to the Divine will in his apostleship (1:1) was probably intended as a signal to them to take everything he wrote seriously as the word of God.

What then are we to make of the assertion often made that the writers of Scripture did not know that they were writing under the inspiration of the Holy Spirit? This is at least too sweeping, as we can see here.

The fact is that apostleship and inspiration go together. When Christ addressed the original apostles shortly before his death, he promised them the Holy Spirit. The Spirit would come to them as the Spirit of Truth to aid them supernaturally in their communication of his truth. These promises are set out in John 14:23-26; 15:26,27; 16:12-15. Paul was not, of course, there at the time, but, as an apostle appointed later by the risen Christ, he would have come into all the good of the promises Jesus gave at this earlier time.

His letters have not lost that authority and need to be taken seriously by us today.

This is underlined by the fact that Paul clearly intended this letter for a wider readership than the particular local church which was its immediate recipient, for he addressed it to 'the church of God in Corinth, together with all the saints through-out Achaia' (v.1; cf. 1 Cor. 1:2). Achaia was a Roman province which had Corinth as its capital.

As we can see in the Acts of the Apostles, Paul and his friends sought to establish strong churches in major centres, such as Thessalonica and Corinth and Ephesus, each of which could then become a base for evangelistic enterprise in its area. It is worth asking if we can learn anything from this strategy today?

We can see here too that local churches had fellowship with each other, and were by no means isolationist. How often today a local church will make decisions and plan enterprises with no thought of seeking co-operation from other like-minded Christian churches!

The addition of Timothy's name is a reminder that this young man joined Paul in his missionary work at Corinth shortly after it commenced (Acts 18:1,5), and in fact Paul alludes to this later in this chapter (1:19). The Corinthian Christians must have known Timothy well, for he had paid another visit to them some time after this (1 Cor. 4:17).

We should not misunderstand the word 'saints' in verse 1. It does not refer to a special class of Christians, but simply to those whom God in Christ has set apart for himself, in other words all Christian believers.

2. His sufferings and comfort (1:3-7)

It is important to notice that Paul begins the body of his letter with praise to God. Quickly he moves on to describe his sufferings, but these in no way modify his praise. In fact, he takes them up fully into his life of worship, for through them he had come to experience the grace of God in new ways, and he wanted to praise him for this. We might well emulate him in this.

There is no suggestion that these sufferings were good in themselves. Paul was no masochist. Rather, he was able to see his sufferings and trials in true perspective because he had discovered how able and willing God was to enable him to endure them.

Does this remind you of the Book of Psalms? In that book, there are praise psalms and there are also laments. Quite often the elements of lament and praise occur together in the same psalm, for the psalmist found that God met him afresh in the context of his trials. Psalm 77 is a good example of this.

There is however a difference between Paul and the psalmists. What they write is very realistic, and we often overhear their complaints to God. Perhaps Paul did go through a stage when he cried out and asked, 'Why is this happening to me?' Being a Christian does not silence all questions, although it does mean that we now have Somebody to whom we can put them. If Paul did complain, however, this was well past by the time he wrote this letter. He was able to do what the psalmist could not yet fully do, because he lived and wrote at an earlier stage of God's revelation, and that was to view his sufferings in the light of the cross.

Difficult experiences often become bearable when we can see some purpose in them. Paul is clearly suggesting here that

God has a very high aim in our experiences of suffering. Through trial, he is seeking nothing less than to reproduce his own character in us.

God is 'the Father of compassion and the God of all comfort, who comforts us in all our troubles' (v. 3). How eloquent these words are!

In the Hungarian National Art Gallery in Budapest, there is a most moving picture. In the foreground are two figures. A young man lies dead upon a bed; beside his body sits his grieving mother. A quick glance at the picture would reveal nothing else. Closer scrutiny, however, discloses the presence of another figure standing unseen in the darkness behind the woman. His presence is shown simply by an arm that has come out of the darkness and is gently placed around her shoulder.

There is an arm, God's arm, that is placed in comfort around the shoulder of every suffering Christian believer.

It is of course an unwritten assumption of what Paul says here, especially in verse 5, that our sufferings should arise out of our obedience to God's will and not in the context of a life of rebelliousness against God in which we are pursuing our own ends (1 Peter 2:20ff.). The comparison between Christ's afflictions and those of Paul and the Corinthians necessarily implies this, for Christ's afflictions were all experienced because God's will for him involved confrontation with sin and evil at many different levels.

Christ's sufferings and ours differ immensely, for his were atoning sufferings, breaking down the barrier between God and ourselves. This we can never do, and thankfully never need to do, as Christ has done this once and for all (2 Cor. 5:18-21).

Nevertheless there are some real comparisons between those sufferings Christ did endure and those that Christians ought to be willing to endure, and most basic of all is a commitment to the will of God even if this involves suffering.

Moreover, we endure such sufferings in living fellowship with Christ himself, which helps us to understand not only this passage, but the words of the risen Christ to a man who was intent on killing his disciples, 'Saul, Saul, why do you persecute me?' (Acts 9:4).

Christ's ministry to us in our afflictions enables us too to exercise a ministry of comfort to others (vv. 5-7). In fact, just as God's revelation may pass through many channels (Rev. 1:1-3), so may his ministry of comfort.

It is of course suffering that makes comfort needful and blessedly appropriate, and it is to the cross, to the 'sufferings of Christ', that we must go for that comfort. Here we find ourselves contemplating the deepest suffering of all and, as Christ's blood was poured out for us, so from its Calvary source comfort, like every other blessing of the Christian life, is outpoured to us.

So there at the cross we discover that suffering, so evil and apparently meaningless in itself, can have eternal significance, for God gives it his own meaning. It was endured for us, for our blessing.

Not only so, but the overflow of Christ's sufferings into our lives becomes in turn an overflow from us to others. Paul is saying that he has realised that, through Christ, his own sufferings may lead to comfort for his Corinthian readers.

What does he mean? It is simply that difficult experiences in which he has received strengthening comfort from God enable him in his turn to minister comfort to other Christians. He can say to them in effect, 'I know that God can give you strength in your trials because he gave me strength in mine.'

How our view of personal suffering is transformed if we see it as God's preparation for a deeper ministry for him on our part!

The result of comfort is 'patient endurance' (v. 6), for the divine remedy is not usually the removal of our afflictions but the imparting of strength to cope with them. It is because Paul has had such experience of the grace of God in his own trials that he can write so confidently of the firm hope he has that God's comforting grace will be the experience of his Corinthian readers too.

3. His sufferings and deliverance (1:8-11)

Although Paul did not find that God removed the element of suffering from his experience, yet he did find him acting in deliverance. This is not contradictory. He is saying that the experience of comfort and strength came first but that in due course it was succeeded by the deliverance.

He writes about particular trials he had endured in the province of Asia (v.8). Did these arise from persecution or from natural factors? The former is the more likely, but we shall probably never know for certain. Again, though, it does not greatly matter, and it may even be of value to us. Its very vagueness means that Christians facing various forms of trial may well feel able to identify with him.

This is sometimes the situation in the psalms, for the writers of them were often up against afflictions of some kinds, and frequently, as for example in Psalm 77, to which we have alluded above, the nature of them is not specified. So, as here, the reader who is in trouble himself may identify with the psalmist and find help from the way the Old Testament believer faced his trials with God.

Paul's experience of pressure was particularly severe and he thought death was near. We might compare the words of Christ spoken in the Garden of Gethsemane, 'My soul is overwhelmed with sorrow to the point of death' (Matt. 26:38).

Paul was brought right to the ultimate limit of his inner resources (v. 9). The purpose of this was to enable him to learn the total reliability of God. Perhaps in this way his conviction, expressed later in this epistle, 'When I am weak, then I am strong' (12:10), was forged for him in the furnace of affliction.

Experience encourages hope. This may not be true of all that people face in life, but it is certainly true of Christian experience. Paul makes this clear elsewhere, in Romans 5:3-5.

Why is this so? It is because it is experience of a God who does not change. Paul looked towards the future, and his hope of deliverance at a later time was based on, or at least strengthened by, his experience that God had delivered him already.

In fact, the whole story of God's dealings with his people recorded in the Bible is often referred to as 'history of salvation', as if that should be thought of as its leading theme. Certainly there is a very full and encouraging record of God's gracious acts of deliverance given in Scripture, culminating of course in the greatest act of all, his deliverance from sin through the atoning death of Jesus.

As we read this history and take in its lessons, this underscores for us the certainty that God's promises of ultimate salvation will be fulfilled in their time, for he is a God of deliverance.

This does not, of course, mean that no Christian will ever have to experience death for Christ's sake, but it does mean that we can look to God to keep us safe from death while he still has work for us to do for him, even though we may have to experience afflictions and trials. Paul certainly had more work ahead of him, and was thankful to be alive to do it.

Yet another dimension of Christian fellowship emerges (v. 11). Paul seeks the prayers of his readers for his personal safety in the ministry God has given him. This shows that even such an outstanding Christian could not do without the prayer support of other Christians in his work for Christ. How we fail if we belong to a local church and benefit from its ministry, and yet never pray for those who minister to us!

Without doubt, Paul's whole outlook was dominated by God, the God who had met him in Christ. It is not simply that he was utterly dependent on him; he was constantly concerned that he should be glorified and praised.

It is not therefore surprising to find him rejoicing in the fact that, when God answers the prayers of the Corinthians and other Christians, he will receive thanks not only from the beneficiaries of those answers but also from those whose prayers have been answered. Both will have plenty of cause to express their thanks to him.

4. Further observations on this passage

Before we leave this opening section of the letter, we should note three things:

First of all, we see that Paul is not simply writing about himself and his sufferings here. He always uses the first person plural. Whatever the trials he faced, Timothy experienced them too. No doubt this joint experience will have given them a spiritual unity in their work which would in its turn bear spiritual fruit – in depth of prayer together, for example.

Note too that Paul has made it very clear that the God of Christ is in fact the Source of every blessing for his people. It is not only the grace and peace of verse 2 but also the comfort and strength of verses 3 to 7 and the deliverance of verses 8 to 11 which come to us from his good hand. In seeing this, we are encouraged to make him our trust in every department of life.

We see also that in the opening section of this epistle, Paul has outlined for us a movement in which blessing comes from God and praise returns to him. God's grace meets us at the cross of Christ, where he suffered for us. As we too experience suffering for Christ's sake, so we are comforted and enabled to bring comfort to other Christians in their afflictions. So this outward movement of grace from God is complemented by the returning prayers and praises of God's people.

Grace from him to us, praise from us to him – these are the twin themes of true Christian living.

Some questions for personal reflection:

1. Can I praise God in the midst of sufferings, and can I give reasons for so praising him?

2. Can my sufferings, by any stretch of imagination, find some parallel in Christ's sufferings, and, if so, what comfort can I take from that?

3. Do I see suffering as a vital part of my training for Christian service in which others may be blessed through me?

4. Am I humble enough to seek the prayers of others for the work God has given me to do and to give full recognition to the fact that their partnership with me through prayer is quite indispensable?

2: SINCERE AND RELIABLE (1:12-22)

Every servant of Christ needs to realize that he or she is sure at some time to be the target of criticism. This may come from the observing world. On the other hand, it may come from the very Christians to whom Christ's servant is called to minister.

Some of this criticism will be deserved. We serve a perfect Christ, but we do not serve him perfectly. Some of it though may well be undeserved.

One of my predecessors as college principal was a man of outstanding godliness. I only ever heard one criticism of him, but I heard it from two different Christians. The allegation was that, although he was greatly respected, he did not sufficiently adopt the style of a man in authority. This was illustrated from the fact that he would never go through a doorway before another person; he always held it open for the other! In other words he was too humble! That 'criticism' said something about him, but it said much more about his critics.

Paul was facing criticism at Corinth. The allegation was that he had promised to visit the church there but had not arrived. How should he deal with this criticism?

There are times when the best thing to do with criticism is simply to commit the whole situation to the Lord and get on with our work. Often we can in fact do some harm to the cause of Christ if we show ourselves to be 'prickly' and resenting criticism. Our pride has been hurt, and that should not be.

There are times however when it is right to offer a defence if we are in a position to do so. What matters – and it is the only thing that matters – is how our testimony for Christ is affected.

This is particularly the case when the issue is truthfulness. We are communicators of the Word of God, and so it is important we do not have a reputation for the misuse of words. This was the situation in which Paul was involved.

1. His conscience (1:12-14)

Here we meet two words that occur fairly frequently in this letter:

Paul says, 'Now this is our boast' (v. 12). Boastfulness is not usually reckoned a Christian virtue, but we should not misunderstand Paul. The fact is that the term has a particular nuance as he uses it in the letter.

The key to this is to be found in 11:16-30, a passage which although very moving also has an element of irony in it. See the comment at that point in the commentary.

Meantime, we note that Paul is saying here that he can look his accusers in the face and declare ('boast') that the charges made against him are false.

It is important too to see that he attributes this personal integrity to God's grace at work in him. This means that his 'boasting' is robbed of all self-centredness. It might well be appropriate, even here, to put the word in inverted commas as the NIV does later on in the epistle. The effect of this is to make the reader stop for a moment and think about the particular use of the word in its context, and this is helpful.

The other word is 'conscience'. This term has a Greek rather than an Old Testament background, but Paul puts it to service for Christ's gospel. It relates to the moral judgment we make on our conscious actions. It has been suggested that the word's prominence in Paul's Corinthian letters may have been due to the fact that it was a favourite word of the Christians there with their Greek background. Sometimes we need to use the words of others, even if they are not the ones we would normally have chosen, in order to get on their wavelength. Critics at Corinth may have condemned him, for reasons that we will soon see, but his conscience, surely influenced by the Spirit of God, has not done so.

This does not mean, of course, that conscience never tells lies, for it needs to be educated by the Word of God, but in

Paul's case the exposure of his conscience to God's truth was very far-reaching and he knew that he had acted with integrity, however it may have appeared to others.

He says that his relations with the Corinthians have been characterized by holiness and sincerity that are from God, rather than by worldly wisdom (vv. 12, 13). This reminds us and would undoubtedly remind them of his discussions of wisdom in chapters 1 to 4 of First Corinthians. There he made it clear that the practical outlook and actions of a Christian should be motivated and directed by a wisdom that cuts right across the world's outlook.

It is not expediency but principle which governs this kind of wisdom, and 'holiness' and 'sincerity' are certainly words indicative of principle. God's grace is the basis of this new wisdom.

What does he mean by this? Probably that when God accepts us freely in Christ, he gives us his Spirit, who begins to shape our outlook in godly ways. To be a Christian is to begin to have a new way of thinking, a new outlook. Paul will show us later (5:16,17) that this new outlook is extremely radical.

He indicates also (v. 13) that his letters did not contain veiled hints so that only the very astute could pick up their meaning, nor did he word them in such a way that they were open to more than one interpretation, so that he was 'hedging his bets'. Some politicians – and others too – could well learn lessons from him!

This should be an encouragement to us in our Bible study. Certainly the Bible contains deep truth, but there is always truth in its surface meaning, and we would not normally expect lengthy, involved explanations of that meaning to be necessary. There is a plainness about the Bible, for it was not written simply for professional theologians but for the ordinary Christian man or woman.

Paul hopes that any lingering qualms the Corinthian Christians may have about him will be fully dispelled and that they could be as proud of him and his ministry as he would be of them when Christ came again, for it is to the second advent that the phrase, 'the day of the Lord Jesus' (v. 14; cf. 1 Cor. 1:8), applies. All Paul's work was done in the light of that coming, when he knew the value of it would be tested (cf. 1 Cor. 3:10-15). To bear this in mind should give seriousness of purpose to all we do.

2. His plans (1:15-17)

These verses clearly suggest that Paul was under attack by some at Corinth for a change of plan. 'Lightly' and 'in a worldly manner' (v. 17) may well have been expressions used by his critics.

When writing First Corinthians, he had outlined travel plans, which clearly included a visit to the church there at Corinth (1 Cor. 16:1-8). Although he had put all this down in black and white, he had evidently not felt able to fulfil this projected itinerary. Hence their criticism and his need to explain.

A comparison of verses 15 to 17 with 1 Corinthians 16 shows that this outline of his plans is a little different from the one set out there. Why is this? Apparently he had decided, after writing the earlier letter, to visit them twice rather than once. He seems to be saying that, far from intending to go back on his promise to them, he had changed his plans in order to benefit them even more fully. If he had in fact fulfilled this second plan, they would surely not have criticised him.

This makes us realize that Paul must have had a strong sense of the strategic importance of the church at Corinth. He was involved in pioneer missionary work in a world nearly all of which was virgin territory as far as the gospel was concerned. Already he had spent 'some time' (Acts 18:18) with the Corinthian Christians on his first visit to their city. Despite this, he had apparently planned to make two visits to them on one missionary journey.

Clearly enough he had a deep concern for the stability and growth in Christ of the Corinthian Christians. Their strategic situation in Achaia and the evangelistic potential it afforded meant, of course, that the blessing they received could flow over from them to others they would themselves influence for Christ. Concentrated work may be more effective than work that extends over a wide area if its result is a fellowship fully equipped and motivated to move out into that wider area in its witness.

After these two visits, so he had planned, they were to send him on his way to Judaea. Probably one of his purposes in going to Corinth would have been to solicit the prayers and support of the Christians there for the Judaean visit. To 'send on my way' may suggest provision as well as valediction (cf. Rom. 15:24), so that it would refer to an all-round act of generous fellowship, but we cannot be sure that the expression was meant to convey as much as this.

We know from chapters 8 and 9 of this letter that Paul attached a lot of importance to this visit to Judaea with money for the support of the Christians there. The money was gathered from various Gentile churches and so it would express the brotherly fellowship between the Gentile Christians who lived in places like Corinth and the Jewish Christians in Jerusalem and Judaea (cf. 1 Corinthians 16:1-4). It would not be surprising then if he regarded the prayer support of the Corinthians for this visit as very important.

In actual fact Paul had not fulfilled this plan, for reasons given later (in 1:23-2:4). Sometimes such alterations in a projected itinerary are unavoidable, and, as we shall see, Paul had a high motive for his delay.

At this point he simply asserts his seriousness of purpose in the plans he had made and his freedom from worldly motivation. Some might have tried to cover themselves against possible changes by being quite vague from the beginning, but this was not Paul's Christian style. He was utterly straightforward and rejected all deviousness.

In our society deviousness has become almost an accepted way of life. Do you always believe the P.A. who says her boss is out of the office when you ring him on a matter you suspect he does not want to discuss with you? The need for a Trade Descriptions Act speaks for itself, as does also the fact that some advertisers seem to be able to get round it! Personal integrity is an essential part of our witness for Christ in modern society.

3. His integrity (1:18-22)

Paul often uses most exalted illustrations, as we can see from passages like Philippians 2:5-11 and 2 Corinthians 10:1, but nowhere is his use of such an illustration more significant than it is here.

In fact, Paul's use of it is so striking, so solemn, that, if he were not telling the truth, his words would be irreverent to the point of blasphemy. He grounds his own claim to truthfulness on the very faithfulness of God himself!

Verse 18 echoes 1 Corinthians 1:9, where also he writes of the faithfulness of God. He had proclaimed a message of truth from the God of Truth, and this message was anything but a mixture of positive and negative. Indeed, it was as positive as could be, for it was in itself an affirmation of the essential faithfulness of the God of the Old Testament who was, above everything else, the God of the promises. This is the way the writers of the New Testament thought of the Old Testament, as a book of Divine promises (cf. e.g. Acts 2:30,31; Heb. 11:11-16). In passage after passage God had made promises to his people, and, in Christ, those promises had been amply fulfilled.

He says that the message of God's faithfulness in Christ was preached not only by him but also by the other members of his team, Silas and Timothy (v. 19). Their presence with him on his first visit to Corinth is confirmed in Acts 18:1-5.

Christ was himself the Theme of their preaching. Paul and the others were not expounding a philosophy or simply advocating a way of life or setting up some new religious sect. They were proclaiming a Person, 'the Son of God, Jesus Christ'.

The term Paul uses most frequently to designate the deity of Jesus is 'Lord', and this occurs with great frequency in his writings. The expression 'Son of God' is nothing like as frequent, but it has been observed that wherever he uses it there is either a certain elevation of his writing style or an exalted topic, or both. This is certainly true here, for Paul is writing about the very character of God.

Christ was not only the great Theme of Paul's preaching. He was that, but he was also the proof that God is true. It would have been possible to demonstrate this on the grand scale, for almost every book of the New Testament bears its own witness to it. A glance through the NIV will show this by the way it presents Old Testament passages in the poetic form characteristic of so many of them, and these passages are quoted there because they are fulfilled in Christ. The Corinthian Christians probably needed no demonstration of this, as it would have been a feature of the preaching of the gospel to them when it first came to Corinth.

In sending Christ, God has said 'Yes!' (v. 20). The preacher of the gospel adds his 'Amen!', which really means 'that is true!' 'Amen' is not a native Greek word but a Hebrew one transliterated, one whose root meaning is 'firm'.

So Paul goes on to say that it is God, the God of Christ, who makes Christians firm and stable (v. 21). This will of course suggest truthful character, personal integrity, but it is probable that Paul's thought goes even beyond this. God gives an all-round spiritual stability and strength to his people. This, Paul recognizes, is shared also by the Corinthian Christians themselves.

Is Paul simply playing with words when he moves from 'Amen' to the firmness it suggests? No, for he is really saying that it is the firmness and stability of the gospel that is the cause of the firmness and stability of the Christian. Relying on the supremely reliable, we become reliable ourselves.

I was once puzzled by the election of a particular student to the student committee of the Christian college where I worked. The students had, however, seen more than I had. I saw rather slender gifts, they saw total reliability, which was undoubtedly caused by strong reliance on God – and they were right!

Because therefore 'Amen!' is a response of the preacher's whole life and that too of his Christian friends, it is very much to the glory of God. That glory of which God had been robbed by human sin (Rom. 3:23) is now restored to him in the characters of his people. That restoration may be imperfect, for we are all imperfect, but it is real.

The words, '... in Christ. He anointed us ...' are very interesting in the Greek, for they read *eis Christon kai chrisas hemas theos* and they contain two words with an obvious connection. *Christos* (of which *Christon* is an inflected form), of course, means 'the anointed One' while *chrisas* means 'anointed'. Paul seems to be saying that something of Christ's anointing by God passes over to and is shared by those who are in Christ.

'Anointing' is a service concept and so this suggests the profound idea, well worth exploring, that the particular service each of us has to engage in arises out of the vocation of Christ, and also that that service can only be fulfilled in that fellowship with Christ which union with him makes possible.

Anointing too has connection with the Holy Spirit, for it

was under his anointing that the Lord Jesus carried out his distinctive work. See especially Hebrews 9:14, where Christ is said to have offered himself without spot to God through the eternal Spirit. Paul will make explicit reference to the Holy Spirit soon.

What a wonderful view of Christian service this is! It suggests both high privilege and immeasurable resources.

And that is not all!

God has also put a seal of ownership on us (v. 22). Paul's language here is based on the commercial practice of the time, and it means that there is some visible evidence that we belong to Christ.

Does this refer, as some think, to baptism as a visible token of our discipleship? Or does it, on the other hand, signify the indwelling of the Spirit (referred to in the context almost immediately) but in terms of the outward evidence of his working in the characters and conduct of the Corinthian believers. Either is possible, but, seeking to understand it in terms of its context, the latter seems the more likely.

The term 'deposit' is also a commercial one. The Greek word *arrabon* was originally Phoenician. A Phoenician trader is selling a commodity, perhaps carpets, but he is unable to supply the quantity needed by a buyer, and so he hands over one. This would have the legal status of a pledge but it would also be a foretaste. It sealed the bargain, was legally accepted as an indication of a binding commercial transaction, and was a foretaste of the rest of the consignment, which could, on its later arrival, be compared with it to make certain the quality was just as high.

How much God has done for us in Christ! In terms of this passage alone, we see that he has given us stability and service, a seal and a surety, plus a present experience of all he intends to give us in the future!

Some questions for personal reflection:

1. Is all my work for Christ carried on in a spirit of complete integrity and truth or do I sometimes bend the truth, perhaps for effect?

2. What are the main spiritual principles I need to keep in mind in any plans I make in my work for the Lord?

3. What place does the faithfulness of God have in the content of the gospel of Christ as I understand it for myself and make it known to others?

4. Am I right to see all that God has done already as a pledge of his ultimate faithfulness?

3: FIRM AND LOVING (1:23-2:13)

We live in a day when 'love' badly needs good Biblical definition. Almost always it is used to designate either sex or sentimentality. In fact, both are capable of existing without any element of real love being present, for love is surely a determination to seek the good of another person. For instance, if we truly love our children, this will involve a measure of discipline, for they are going to have to face life in the real world.

There is something quite special about Christian love, for, as Paul makes so clear to us in Romans 8:28, 29, our good means our likeness to Christ. So if real Christian love is concerned about this, it will not pander to every whim of those who are loved, for this kind of treatment can be ruinous to character. If we are never told our faults, we are unlikely to seek the grace of God for putting them right.

If a merely sentimental approach to loving others is wrong, this is just as true when the object of love is a church. A faithful preacher of the Word of God will certainly encourage his listeners when this is appropriate, but he will not be constantly patting them on the back. Both faithfulness to God and love for them will require him to speak sternly to them at times when this is necessary.

1. Pastoral Motivation (1:23-2:4)
For the second time in this chapter, Paul invokes the name of God, but not this time for purposes of comparison as in verse 18. Strictly translated, what he is saying is 'I call God as witness against my life'. This is very solemn indeed, for he is really saying that if he is lying God should take his life.

Paul's change of plan which, as we have seen from 1:15-17, was not imaginary but real, had a pastoral reason. It had nothing whatever to do with personal expediency, but in fact was

48

determined by his love for the Corinthian Christians. How hurt-
ful their criticism of him was, in view of this!

The apostle was no tyrant, not even a benevolent dictator, a
'heavy shepherd' (v. 24). His ministry to them always called for
their co-operation, and he sought for this. He was so eager to work
with them for their blessing. We can see this in all his letters.

This is in fact the purpose of ministry. It does not impose, it
seeks voluntary response. Certainly authentic Christian ministry does rest on Biblical authority, but it never proceeds by au-
thoritarianism nor by brainwashing. It seeks the free co-operation of those Christ has set free to serve him.

Paul's reference to 'your joy' may be eschatological, that is,
a reference to the joy they will have when Christ returns, or he
may have in mind their present experience of joy in God. Probably both are in view, although 2:3 makes it seem likely that the
emphasis is on the latter.

'It is by faith you stand firm', he says. It is important to
compare this with the comment he makes in 1:21. When we do
this, we conclude that it is God who makes us firm, who gives
us stability, but that in fact he does this through our faith, not
without it. Once again, Paul is making it clear that on the human side what is so necessary is simple trust in God.

This is a consistent principle of the sanctifying work of the
Holy Spirit. He does not work round the back of us, but through
us. In the nature of things, this must be so, for his work affects
our characters, and character, although manifesting itself in outward actions, is in fact something that is deeply rooted in our
inner life.

This passage is a key one for reconstructing the history of
Paul's dealings with the Corinthian church. This history is somewhat complex and the table on page 25 gives the most likely
order of the events, including both the painful visit and painful
letter referred to here.

It is quite evident that Paul's pastoral firmness was mani-
fested both in person and on paper. This gives the lie to the
assertion made by his opponents that, although he could write
strong things from a distance, he could not act in accordance
with them when face to face with the Corinthian Christians
themselves (10:10).

Christian fellowship involves the sharing of the deep experiences and profound emotions of life with other believers. Just
as he had wanted them to share the comfort he was given in his
sufferings (1:3-11), so he was eager for them also to share his
joy (2:4). This joy was specifically related to their condition as
Christian disciples. He found joy in seeing the work of God in
their characters. Christian joy is not in fact a self-centred quality at all, for we find our joy in Christ and in those in whom
Christ's character is revealed.

Paul's distress had been very great (2:4), not only in terms
of visible tears but also the invisible motions of his heart. So
many people, and even Christians, have quite a wrong image of
Paul. There was nothing of the aloof rationalist about him; he
was a man of great emotional depth, and in this way reflected
something of the character of his Lord, the God who was incar-
nate in Christ.

The word 'love' is most emphatic. Love makes us vulner-
able, for it opens us to other people. Paul's deep distress was in
fact caused by deep love. This was his real motive, the fatherly
and motherly concern of which he writes in 1 Thessalonians
2:7-12.

One word group is very prominent in these opening verses
of chapter 2, and its prominence continues as far as verse 7.
The NIV translates it by 'painful', 'grieve', 'grieved', 'distressed', 'sorrow'.

The basic idea is simply pain. This gives the lie to the view,
rarely spelled out but sometimes tacitly assumed, that the Chris-

tian may know a virtually pain-free existence, as if Christ's sal-vation removed us from trials and difficulties. The pain of the Corinthians was their own fault, but this was certainly not true of Paul's pain, for it arose out of deep concern for them.

2. Productive discipline (2:5-11)

It is not quite certain to whom Paul is referring in these verses. It looks as though he has one particular person in mind, al-though this is not quite certain from the way he expresses him-self ('if anyone', v. 5) here.

If one person is in view, many commentators have taken it that this is a reference to the incestuous man about whom he wrote to the Corinthians in 1 Corinthians 5. In that case, the reference to sorrow (v.7) suggests that the man concerned has shown genuine repentance, and that Paul is here counselling the Corinthian Christians to restore him to their fellowship. The fact that Paul had written to them about the matter (v.9) would link up well with this, for it is quite natural to assume this was in First Corinthians.

There is, however, another possibility, and this is argued by other commentators. There were people at Corinth who had been working against Paul. He is perhaps thinking here in general terms about such people or he may have one in particular, per-haps a leader of the group, in mind. Paul's references to his own forgiveness of this man, even though he plays down the wrong done to him somewhat, would suggest this interpretation. In this case, perhaps the reference to writing is in fact to the pain-ful letter of verse 4 and not to 1 Corinthians 5.

It is possible to make out a case for either interpretation, but the context fits the second better. This is because Paul is aware here of criticism directed against him personally, so that these verses would cohere well with the general context if the second interpretation be correct.

The man has caused grief to the Corinthians. When there has been very evident sin in a member of a Christian fellowship, it is the depth of grief which will show the spiritual depth of that fellowship. If there is an element of pride in the members, a 'holier than thou' attitude, then it is most doubtful if there is a deep work of the Holy Spirit in the people. The Holy Spirit is grieved by sin (Eph. 4:30; cf. Isa. 63:10) and this shows his love as well as his holiness. His controlling presence in a local church will make it a deeply loving fellowship and so this will find its expression in grief in the members in such a circumstance.

It is evident that Paul feels that God's purpose in the act of discipline has now been fulfilled. It seems clear from verse 7 that the man who was at fault must have shown signs of genuine repentance. There has been a fulfilment in their obedience to what Paul had exhorted them to do (v.9). Perhaps there had at first been reluctance to impose discipline. This was certainly the case if the man concerned was the incestuous person of 1 Corinthians 5.

What steps then are they to take? They are to forgive him (vv.7,8). The references to comforting him and reaffirming their love to him mean that their forgiveness is to be full and final. It is to be a true expression of love and therefore to lead to a completely restored fellowship.

Paul too has forgiven him (v.10). Why was this necessary? It is easy to understand if he was prominent among those who had been working against Paul, but on either view of his identity he had clearly caused him a lot of anguish. What for many commentators is decisive in favour of the 'opponent' theory and against the 'incestuous man' theory is Paul's comment, 'if there was anything to forgive'. It is a positive character mark to play down an offence against ourselves, but definitely a negative one to dismiss lightly an offence which is not only against

God but which involves grievous harm to another person, an offence such as incest.

He says that he has forgiven the man 'in the sight of Christ for your sake'. What does this mean? His forgiveness has been from the heart, which of course is seen by the all-seeing Christ (cf. Hebrews 4:13), and it is for their sake so that the breach in the fellowship made by the act of discipline can be quickly mended.

Without doubt Satan would want this wound in the life of the local church to remain unhealed as long as possible (v.11). Grief in a church in such a situation is absolutely right, but it is bound to make it somewhat introspective for a while. An introspective church is unlikely to be an evangelizing church, and this must please the Evil One. So it is for the benefit of the work of God for matters like this to be cleared up before too much time has elapsed.

Paul says, 'we are not unaware of his schemes'. Perhaps 'we' here applies to himself and Timothy (1:1). In their work of proclaiming the gospel and establishing local churches they must often have encountered the schemes of Satan, for their work was to be strategic in overcoming him.

It is unwise for us simply to repeat Paul's words here, applying them to ourselves, without considering whether they are really true of us. We have need of God-given wisdom if we are to see and understand the ploys of Satan, but this is a spiritual quality we may humbly seek from the Lord. In *The Screwtape Letters*, C. S. Lewis shows insight into Satan's ways when he shows him seeking to cloke his activities.

3. Postponed evangelism (2:12,13)

For the background to these verses, see Acts 19:21,22; 20:1-6. This was Paul's second visit to Troas, for it was there that a most significant event had taken place earlier in his missionary work, when a man of Macedonia had appeared to him in a vision and he had moved into Europe with the gospel (Acts 16:8-10).

These verses may surprise the Christian reader somewhat. If Paul had found an opening for the gospel in Troas and if he was fully persuaded that God had himself given him this opening, why did he let anything deter him from exploiting it fully? His commitment to the gospel was total and he would never normally lose an opportunity of proclaiming it.

Is the answer simply that Paul was human, and that there were times when he failed to do the right thing? Certainly we should not regard the apostles as perfect witnesses for Christ. Their teaching was infallible, for they spoke and wrote under the inspiration of the Holy Spirit, but only Christ was perfect in life and character. Is it possible that Paul felt the need of support by Titus so much that he put this before the needs of preaching? This is not impossible, but it seems unlikely.

After all, if this was what happened, we might expect Paul to introduce a note of self-criticism into what he says here. He was so sensitive as a Christian that it is most unlikely his Christian conscience would not have troubled him if he had been guilty of dereliction of duty, and he was so frank and open in his letters that he would probably have said so.

It is, in fact, important to note that the passage does not say that he did not preach the gospel there, although it does suggest curtailment of plans to do so. This might have been justifiable for good Christian reasons, as we will suggest.

Why his lack of peace? There could have been more than one reason. Titus was a member of his team and he may have been concerned for his safety. A responsible leader must always have a pastoral concern for his team members. Also he was deeply concerned about the situation at Corinth and probably found it difficult to concentrate until he got news of it. If so, this certainly shows he was a normal human being. Later on, after a staggering catalogue of his sufferings, he says, 'Besides everything else, I face daily the pressure of my concern for all the churches' (2 Cor 11:28). To him this was no small thing, for the context in chapter 11 suggests that it caused him no little suffering.

The tension that may be set up for a Christian worker between his evangelistic and his pastoral concerns is not always easy to resolve. Of course, godly planning will make space for both, but there are times when one or other has the larger claim. Paul's assessment of priorities here may have also taken account of the fact that local churches are themselves meant to be centres of evangelism, so that he was promoting an evangelistic as well as a pastoral aim in going on to Macedonia and thence, of course, to Corinth.

Some questions for further reflection:

1. Should I be prepared to change plans, even if I have made these prayerfully, if I see the desirability of this for spiritual ends?

2. Are firmness and discipline denials of love or functions of it?

3. What kind of evidence does true penitence reveal in the person who demonstrates it?

4. Can Satan use for his own ends men and women who have been touched by the grace of God, and, if so, how can we avoid being so used by him?

4: CELEBRATING
AND COMMUNICATING (2:14-3:6)

We have reached a very significant place in Paul's letter to the Corinthian church, for this is where the so-called 'Great Digression' begins.[1]

You may have noticed, in reading his epistles, that he moves away at times from his main argument and writes for a little while about some other issue, before returning to his main line of thought again. This is a characteristic of his style.

Notice, for example, how often this happens in his letter to the Ephesians. The NIV helps us, because it places a dash after 3:1, and this indicates a digression which continues until Paul gets back to his main line of thought at verse 14. This phenomenon usually seems to occur when he pens a word or phrase that fires his imagination. His heart becomes so filled with wonder and praise that he simply must put into writing the thoughts that have been evoked by that wonder.

Incidentally, this shows us that the Holy Spirit's inspiration of a Bible writer did not bypass his feelings but worked through his whole personality.

The digression here, by far the longest to be found in Paul's writings, does not end until 7:4. Its subject is the Christian ministry, its principles and its practice. It was a subject which filled his heart with amazed wonder, because he knew that his own work as a preacher of the gospel was entirely due to God's mercy and unmerited favour towards him (4:1; cf. Eph. 3:7ff.; 1 Tim. 1:12-14). 'Once a persecutor of the Christians and now a preacher of Christ's gospel – what almost unbelievable grace!' he must have thought.

This part of his letter is immensely valuable for anybody

---

1. See Introduction, p. 22.

doing Christian work, whether a pastor or missionary, a Sunday school teacher or youth club leader, or a Christian seeking to witness for Christ in his home or place of work. This means of course that it is of real value for any Christian, as we are all called to Christian service.

1. Christ's triumphal procession (2:14-16)

As we have already seen, after his opening greetings, Paul commenced his letter with an ascription of praise to God (1:3ff.). He now begins to praise the Lord again. The subject of his thanksgiving is quite different this time, however, for it is not about comfort in suffering but rather triumph in ministry.

He uses a most striking analogy based on Roman military practice. The Greek word *thriambeuein* translated 'leads ... in triumphal procession' (v. 14) is the key to this. Let's look at its background.

A Roman general has won a notable victory over the enemies of Rome. He makes contact with the Senate in Rome, and asks leave to have an official triumph. If this is granted, he will proceed with his victorious troops and with his notable captives to a spot some miles from the capital city, and there arrange all the personnel in order.

He will of course be leading the way, riding in his ceremonial chariot. Behind him will come his victorious troops and also the captives who will be going to their execution.

This general picture of a triumph we can gather from Roman sources. It is known too that sacrifices would be offered to the gods when the procession reached its destination. Less certain, but very likely, is the fact that in the procession, perhaps near its front, there were people scattering incense, so that its fragrance would herald the arrival of the victorious general.

Paul uses this kind of event as a vehicle for his thought. Murray Harris expresses the matter very well when he says,

'The metaphor is certainly suggestive: Christ undertook a bat-
tle not rightly his; we share in a triumph not rightly ours.' It
may be that Paul is here employing an illustration he often used
in his preaching of the gospel.

In this context, the triumphal procession must represent the
progress of the gospel of Christ. How does this connect up with
the verses that precede this illustration? He appears to be saying that, despite his change of plan, the gospel continues to
progress, and so in this way God has over-ruled the situation
for his glory.

Are the followers of Christ pictured here as his victorious
troops or as vanquished foes? Commentators are somewhat divided, for there is no doubt that both views can be supported,
although the majority opinion is that it is the victorious troops
Paul has in mind.

The word *thriambeuein* occurs once more in the New Testament, in Colossians 2:15, where we see how Christ demonstrates
his victory over his foes at the cross. The foes there are the
spiritual powers and authorities, the hosts of Satan. It does not
seem likely therefore that Paul would apply the same picture
quite differently here, picturing Christians as defeated foes, even
if he did think of them as now willingly taking their place as
Christ's captives. So it is likely he thinks of Christians as sol-
diers in Christ's army, sharing in his glorious triumph.

How do Paul and the members of his evangelistic team figure in terms of the illustration? If in fact there were incense-
scatterers employed in the Roman triumphs, then this is the
role of the preachers of the gospel.

If the incense bearers proceeded ahead of the general to signal his imminent arrival, does this suggest that the preaching
prepares for the Second Advent? Attractive as this interpretation is, we cannot be sure this is Paul's meaning.

The incense of the gospel has a most delightful smell, for it is in fact 'the aroma of Christ'. It would be a mistake to identify this simply with the verbal message of the gospel. Paul says, 'We are to God the aroma of Christ', so that we see it is not simply the message but the messengers who are Christ's aroma, for they reveal his character.

Did the poet perhaps have this passage in mind when he wrote,

> As some rare perfume in a vase of clay
> Pervades it with a fragrance not its own,
> So when Thou dwellest in a human soul,
> All heaven's own sweetness seems around it thrown'?

There are circumstances in life when something intrinsically attractive ceases to allure us because of its associations. If a parent were foolish enough to put on a record of beautiful music each time he administered unmerited punishment to a child, the child would come to hate the music as much as the punishment.

The gospel is the most attractive message ever to be heard by human ears. The man or woman who rejects the gospel and the Christ of that gospel may however view the message with distaste or regard it as being like a nauseating odour. This is because it challenges a person's whole way of life, it demands that sin be faced, it calls for repentance. How different though is its smell to those whose response is full-hearted and believing!

When Paul uses the phrase, 'to God' (v. 15), he may also have in mind the burnt-offerings of the Old Testament which are described in Leviticus as 'an aroma pleasing to the LORD' (Lev. 1:9), because they showed the obedience of his people.

It is not surprising that Paul cried out, 'Who is equal to such a task?' The task is so holy and the issues of it so solemn that such a response is natural. In fact it is to be expected.

2. Christ's sincere messenger (2:17)

Paul had been into a number of Greek cities with the gospel before he arrived at Corinth. When seeking for a good place to stand and proclaim the good news about Jesus, he would no doubt encounter many other open-air speakers whose main interest seemed to be in money rather than in truth.

Justin Martyr, the second century Christian apologist, went the rounds of the philosophical teachers in Ephesus in a search for truth prior to his conversion to Christ. He found them all wanting, and mentions that among them was one who asked for his fee far too early. This may have been a common experience.

Paul never asked for money for preaching the gospel. He was certainly willing to accept financial support from his fellow-Christians, but payment from the evangelized was quite another matter (11:7-9). After all, the gospel itself proclaims free forgiveness and it should be given freely (cf. Matt. 10:8).

The word translated 'peddle', is to be found only here in the New Testament, although it does occur once in the Septuagint, the main Greek version of the Old Testament available in New Testament times. It suggests a distinctly low type of trader, and shows that Paul viewed such peddling of the gospel as contemptible.

No doubt such traders had a touch of the confidence trickster about them, using smooth talk to sell rubbish at unreasonable prices. The Christian evangelist is not plying a nefarious trade, nor does he do his work to feather his own nest; he is sent by God. He does not employ trickery, but speaks out of a sincere heart, for he is conscious that he is speaking, not only in the presence of his hearers but of the God who has sent him.

'To God (v.15) ... before God ... from God...' Paul was conscious that everything he did was to be done in a highly responsible and God-honouring manner.

Here was great challenge, but there was also great encouragement, for he and his companions bore their witness not only 'to God' but 'in Christ' (cf. v. 14). Somebody who is working for Christ has, in virtue of his union with Christ, great spiritual resources.

3. Christ's personal letter (3:1-3)
What does Paul mean when he says, 'Are we beginning to commend ourselves again?'

The writing of letters of introduction or commendation has been a common practice in many societies and this was certainly true of the Classical world. It was a guarantee of the authenticity of the claims made by strangers.

The New Testament shows evidence that, in addition to the normal run of unscrupulous imposters, there were false teachers about who were masquerading as authentic Christian instructors (2 Peter 2; 1 John 4:1; 2 John 7-11; Jude 4-19).

We all have a certain healthy fear of being imposed on by strangers who are in fact charlatans, and yet we do not want to turn an unwelcoming face to every fresh person we meet. The letter of introduction solves this particular social dilemma, although these days it may be replaced by a call on the telephone.

Perhaps some of his critics at Corinth were saying that he and his friends had arrived in the city with no backing from others. In the eyes of these critics, their unheralded arrival would be tantamount to self-commendation.

These Corinthian critics may have had something in common with those who appear to have said at Galatia that he was simply a representative of the 'real' apostles in Jerusalem and that he had gone beyond his brief from them. This is normally inferred from Paul's vigorous defence of his independence and direct call from God penned in Galatians, chapters 1 and 2.

Just as Paul has earlier used the illustration of the Roman triumph (2:14-16), so now he draws spiritual truth out of the commending letter. He asserts that he and his fellow-workers need no literal letter, for they have a figurative one, full of evidence of their authenticity as genuine messengers of Christ. This 'letter' consists in fact of the believers at Corinth themselves and it comes from Christ, for apart from him and his gospel this evidence would not exist.

Who then was the scribe used by Christ to pen this 'letter'? It was Paul and his travelling companions considered collectively.

What ink was used so that the message could be clearly read? This was the Holy Spirit, whose work in the Corinthian Christians was so articulate. He had imparted new life to them (3:6), making increasing character likeness to Christ a real possibility (3:18). In 1 Corinthians 12-14, while Paul recognized the charismatic work of the Spirit, he had emphasized in chapter 13 the supreme importance of love in a passage that reminds us very much of the character of Christ.

What writing material was used? Was it tablets of stone? No, it was human hearts, for the Corinthians did not experience a superficial reformation but a deep inner change. Even so, the letter could be read by others for, Paul was clearly implying, what had been done in their hearts inevitably showed in their conduct.

The ancient manuscripts vary as to whether they read 'your hearts' or 'our hearts' in verse 2, but the latter is a little more likely to be the true text than the former. If so, then, by using the first person plural, Paul is probably again underlining his sincerity and that of his companions. A written communication always begins in the mind and heart of its author before it finds written form. The letter Paul and his friends had written ended by being read by others, as the lives of the converts were open to inspection, but it started in the hearts of the writers and proceeded through their sincere preaching of Christ's gospel.

Let us note too that he does not write of 'letters' but of a 'letter' (vv. 2,3). His use of the singular here testifies to his churchmanship. It was not simply the conversion of individuals that showed the authenticity of the gospel messengers, but the establishment of a church, a godly society within an ungodly one.

4. Christ's dependent ministers (3:4-6)

Does it seem as if Paul has been making too great a claim? Perhaps he felt that some of his readers might think so. Perhaps they would think this to be unjustified boasting on his part. For this reason, he underlines the fact that he and the other members of his evangelistic team are utterly dependent on God in Christ for all they are and do.

Their confidence is 'through Christ' (v. 4), for without him they are nothing. It is also 'before God', for they are very conscious that all they do is done in his holy presence.

In 2:16, Paul, deeply aware of the seriousness of the gospel ministry, cries out, 'And who is equal to this task?' The NIV obscures the fact that he uses the same adjective there and in verses 5 and 6 here where it is translated 'competent'.

Placing these verses together, we see that he is stating two great complementary principles of Christian service, indeed of the whole Christian life. What is asked of us is beyond us, so that a profound acceptance of and confession of our total inability is not only appropriate but is called for. Does this mean then that the task before us is impossible in an absolute sense? No, for God supplies us with infinite resources.

Total inability in ourselves, total ability in Christ – it is doubtful whether anything more important than this can ever be said about our life and work as Christians.

It is vital for us to keep these two principles in balance. An awareness of our total inability without a grasp of the great resources we have in Christ will lead us only to despair. On the other hand, great confidence in God which is not balanced by a sense of personal inadequacy may well pass over gradually into self-confidence, as we come to imagine that what is God's doing is really our own.

These principles find striking illustration in the story of the call of the fishermen-disciples in Luke 5. As the miraculous draught of fishes was hauled into the boat, Simon Peter 'fell at Jesus' knees and said, "Go away from me, Lord; I am a sinful man." ... Then Jesus said to Simon, "Don't be afraid; from now on you will catch men"' (Luke 5:8, 10). In Mark 1:17, he is recorded as saying, 'I will make you fishers of men.'

Even though made competent, we are not made independent. The word *diakonos* translated 'ministers' (v. 6) is the ordinary Greek word for a servant, which, unlike *doulos* ('slave'), covered all servants, both bond and free. Of course, every servant is under authority in the performance of his service, so that we are not freelance workers but are under the authority of Christ.

We serve Christ in relation to the New Covenant. This expression calls to mind an extensive range of Old Testament teaching plus that of Christ himself.

Covenant is a most important theme in the Old Testament; in fact some regard it as the most important of all. It is a relationship word, and in Old Testament times could cover anything from a treaty between nations to a promise of faithful friendship between two people. Most important though is its use of the relations between God and people, notably the nation of Israel.

'New' of course implies the existence of what is old. The key passage for understanding this is Jeremiah 31:31-34 and this should be consulted. The covenant God made with the fore-fathers of the Israelites of Jeremiah's day was the one instituted so solemnly at Sinai, with its emphasis on the Law, written on tablets of stone. This the people broke, not just once but time and time again, when they sinned against God.

Instead of casting them away, which was certainly their desert, God promised a New Covenant. This would be much more inward than the Old, for God's Law would now be written on people's hearts, and it was more personal than the Old, for it would give personal knowledge of God. It also gave forgiveness, so necessary when the Old Covenant had been so seriously broken.

Now Paul writes, of course, against a background of first-century Pharisaism, which tended to harden the Mosaic Law into a system of self-salvation. As Paul himself points out in Galatians, the result of this is condemnation, for the Law judges adversely all who try to justify themselves in God's eyes through keeping it (Gal. 3:10-12).

This then explains Paul's references here to the letter and to the Spirit. This has sometimes been understood as a reference to literal versus spiritual interpretation of the Bible. In fact it has nothing whatever to do with this, but everything to do with seeking to achieve salvation under the Old Covenant versus receiving it as a gift under the New.

Paul's reference to the Spirit here will call to mind another key Old Testament passage, for Ezekiel says that God would put his Spirit in the hearts of his people (Ezek. 36: 26, 27). It is therefore through the Spirit that the Law is engraved on the hearts of God's people.

It is possible to live on this side of Christ and yet still to have an Old Covenant attitude, or, perhaps more accurately, a Pharisaic one. What is salvation to me? Is it something to be earned by my own poor efforts, or is it a wonderful free gift from God that leads me to do his will so gratefully from the heart and in the power of his Spirit?

Some questions for further reflection:

1. Do I see the progress of the gospel in the world as a celebration of the victory of Christ?

2. Do I make clear to those to whom I bear witness for Christ that the consequences of rejecting the gospel message are extremely serious?

3. It has been well said that the church is the only Bible many people will ever read. How convincing a letter to the 'reading' world is your church?

5: A WONDERFUL
NEW RELATIONSHIP (3:4-18)

No reader of the New Testament can move through many of its chapters without realizing how intimately it is related to the Old. This is true in general terms for the whole New Testament. There are however some passages where it is particularly evident, for they consist almost entirely of Christian comment on an Old Testament event or institution or theme.

This is certainly true here, for without a knowledge of important events in the life of Moses these verses cannot be understood at all. We will need therefore to remind ourselves of that background before we look at the passage in detail.

Moses was appointed by God to be the mediator of the Old Covenant, that is, to represent God to Israel and Israel to God when God met his people at Mount Sinai, the place where, by God's initiative, the Old Covenant relationship was made (Deut. 5:1-5). Moses went up that mountain and into the presence of God to receive the Law from him, while the people remained at a distance (Exod. 20:18-21; 24:1-2).

When he came down again, his face was aglow with radiant light. This was due to his sojourn in God's presence. The Israelites were scared when they saw his face, and so Moses placed a veil over it and he kept it there all the time he was in the camp of Israel. When he went back up the mountain into God's presence again he removed this veil (Exod. 34:29-35).

The Jews of New Testament times were extremely interested in Moses and everything concerning him, for it was through him that God had given the Law to Israel. We can be sure therefore that the Christians at Corinth who were Jews or who, as Gentiles interested in Judaism, had worshipped at the local synagogue, would know this story very well. Paul uses it to illustrate differences between the Old and New Covenants, the Old made through Moses and the New through Christ.

It is possible too that Paul had in mind another mountain and another shining face, the Mount of Transfiguration and the glory that came, not just from the face but from the whole bodily presence of Christ there (Luke 9:28-36). There is no express reference to this in the passage, but the reader familiar with that story finds himself constantly reminded of it.

Paul had not been on the Transfiguration Mount, but he had met Christ in all his radiant glory on the Damascus Road (Acts 9:1-9). No doubt this experience too will have coloured his language here.

Certainly it is 'glory' that unites all these stories and also provides Paul with one of his two key words for this section. What does it mean?

The Greek word is *doxa*. In the Septuagint (the Greek version of the Old Testament used in New Testament times), it is used to translate the Hebrew *kabod*, which originally meant 'weight', and so came to be used of what was substantial in other ways. Perhaps because there is no 'weightier' subject than God himself it then came to be employed of the disclosure of the 'weightiness' of God's revelation of himself. It is not precisely a synonym for God, but rather for God as he has graciously shown himself to us, to human beings. There may be more to God than he has shown us, but what he has shown us is his glory.

Yet another idea came to be attached to it, that of *light*. God is said, in the Old Testament, to wrap himself in light (Ps. 104:2), and in the New to dwell in unapproachable light (1 Tim. 6:16). There is something of a paradox here, for this light therefore both reveals and conceals him.

Significance (i.e. weight), revelation, outshining light, all these ideas attach to this great word here.

The other key word is 'ministry'. Already he has said that God has made us 'ministers of a new covenant' and 'minister' means 'servant'. How then is the New Covenant served? In a variety of ways, but primarily by being proclaimed, for it is a message.

The Old Covenant had its messengers in Paul's day, for, as James said at the important Council of Jerusalem, referring to the presence of synagogues not only in Israel but in many other places, 'Moses has been preached in every city from the earliest times and is read in the synagogues on every Sabbath' (Acts 15:21).

Now Paul, and in fact Christians generally, had been given the privilege of spreading the gospel of the New Covenant, the new and deeper relationship with human beings God has graciously made possible through Christ.

1. A greater glory (3:7-11)

These verses describe the contrast, and yet at the same time the comparison, between the two great covenants. It is not in fact possible to contrast usefully two things or ideas which have nothing in common. How can you contrast Buckingham Palace and three o'clock? It is because both covenants reveal God and so have glory, and also because both are declared through preaching, that they can be compared.

It might seem a little surprising at first that Paul does not compare and contrast the two covenants in sacrificial terms, with the oft-repeated sacrifices of animals being contrasted with the once-for-all sacrifice of Christ. This is what the Epistle to the Hebrews does in its tenth chapter. Instead Paul concentrates on the work of the Spirit rather than on Christ's work.

Why does he do this? Because the Pharisees, whose outlook controlled most Jewish thinking in his day, tended to emphasize the outward law rather than the inner motive. The Judaizers, who were affected by Pharisaic theology and who stressed the importance of circumcision[1], had something of the same tendency. It was important therefore to stress the Spirit's work

1. See Introduction, p. 15.

in order to underline the inwardness of the gospel. The Old Covenant was engraved on stones, the Second involves a work of the Spirit in the heart.

This also fitted in with his earlier illustration of the letter and with the fact that God had witnessed to the authenticity of his own ministry by changing the hearts of those who responded to his message (3:1-3).

The Old Covenant brings death, whereas the New brings life (v.7, cf. v.6). Death comes through the Old, of course, because the Law imposes conditions which we cannot fulfil because of our sinfulness (Gal. 3:10-12). The New Covenant, on the other hand, brings eternal life in Christ.

Closely connected with the ideas of death and life are those of condemnation and righteousness (v.9). Why is this? Because God condemns sin and death is the penalty of sin (Gen. 2:17), while life is the consequence of receiving righteousness through what Christ has done for us (Rom 5:18).

So then, Paul is suggesting, the glory of God is much more fully revealed under the New Covenant because the Old revealed his judgment while the New his grace, although he does not use that actual word here.

Does this mean that there was no experience of God's grace under the Old Covenant? Not necessarily, for elsewhere Paul not only sees the pre-Mosaic Abraham as experiencing God's grace through faith (Rom. 4) but also the post-Mosaic David (Rom. 4:6-8). The principles of salvation by grace are, however, much more fully and more clearly revealed now through Christ. In any case, it is the legal factor in the Old Covenant, which is prominent in the story of Moses, with which he is concerned here.

The very term 'New Covenant', of course, clearly implies that the former covenant has been replaced, as the Epistle to the Hebrews, quoting from Jeremiah, argues from his use of the term (Heb. 8:7-13).

Paul sees a symbol of its supercession in the story of Moses too. He infers from Exodus 34 that the glory must have been fading from the face of Moses while the veil was covering it and until such time as that radiance was renewed when he went again into God's presence. Here then is a picture, a kind of acted prophecy, of the fading away of the Old Covenant (vv. 7,11,13).

Paul makes it clear too that there can be no question of the New Covenant being replaced, for its glory is 'the glory of that which lasts' (v. 11). This shows that in this covenant God has accomplished all that needed to be done.

Throughout all this, of course, he does recognize that there was a revelation, a glory, in the Old Covenant too, even though it was less than that of the New. To assert the unsurpassed glory of the sun is not to deny the glory of the moon.

2. A veiled glory (3:12-15)

Paul, still having in mind the story of Moses and the Old Covenant, now seems to be thinking of his own proclamation of the gospel of the New Covenant, and particularly of those occasions when he had done so in the Jewish synagogues.

Because the glory of the New Covenant is a lasting one, the Christian has great hope as far as the future is concerned (v. 12). The future is secure because God has secured it for us by establishing this covenant for us and with us.

It is this strong and certain hope that Paul shares with his fellow-preachers, and it gives them great boldness as they declare the gospel. After all, there is nothing tentative or unsure about the hope they have in Christ, so why should they preach tentatively? Their preaching is given a boldness which befits it. This surely still applies!

Paul saw contrast between the boldness of the Christian preacher and the veiling of the face of Moses (v. 13), himself the original preacher of the Old Covenant. The Israelites would have been amazed if they had seen how the glory was fading away under Moses' veil and had understood its significance. How astonishing that a covenant given in the dramatic circumstances of Sinai should in fact have been destined to pass away and to be replaced by another, but it was true!

We need to remember that 'glory' is God revealed. So the bright face of Moses made the people afraid, for there is something awesome about the revelation of a God who is holy. This was the God whose presence at Sinai caused it to 'blaze with fire to the very heavens, with black clouds and deep darkness' (Deut. 4:11) and who had made known what he required of his people in an audible voice nobody who heard it would ever forget (Exod. 19:19-20:21).

For Paul the external veil symbolised an inner dullness of mind (v. 14). Clearly this was spiritual, not simply intellectual. In what did it consist? He does not say, but a little later on he tells his readers that the gospel of the glory of Christ is veiled to unbelievers (4: 3,4). So here he must mean that the Law could have shown them more than it did, and that the cause of its failure to do this was something in them, not something in the Law itself.

Certainly in Romans 3:21,22, he says plainly that both the Law and the Prophets witness to the good news that God has provided righteousness in Christ. Our Lord, too, marvelled that the two disciples who conversed with him on the road to Emmaus were so slow at heart and had not understood what the Law and the Prophets had said about him (Luke 24:25-27).

The veil had meaning for Paul's own day as well as for the time of Moses. He discovered its continuing presence during the course of his evangelistic preaching in the synagogues (vv. 14b-16), and the adverse attitude of many of the Jews to the Christian message is documented by Luke (Acts 13:44-46; 17:1-5; 18:5,6).

Paul writes of reading the Old Covenant, or of reading Moses (vv. 14,15). So he treats the Old Covenant here as a body of literature, and this is appropriate for it is in what we call the Old Testament that the Old Covenant is exhibited.

There has been no reference to Christ since verse 4. Now, however, he tells of the removal of the veil 'in Christ'. This was, of course, his own experience, on the Damascus Road and in the days that followed his encounter with Christ there. His eyes had a darkness they had never known before (Acts 22:6-11), but his heart was flooded with light, a light he was told to pass on to others (Acts 26:15-19).

Although many of his fellow-Jews had rejected the gospel, he had also seen the veil removed as others had received the good news of Jesus Christ he had been sent to proclaim to them (Acts 13:43; 17:4, 10-12).

3. An increasing glory (3:16-18)
At first sight, the thought of verse 16 seems virtually identical with that of verse 14b. In fact, it is not, for 'in Christ' and turning to 'the Lord', although related, are not identical in this particular passage. The latter expression is drawn from the story of Moses, while the former is not.

As we have seen, it was when Moses again went up the mountain and turned to the Lord that the veil was removed from his face (Exod. 34:34,35). He did this deliberately, of course, and there is a deliberateness in the turning to the Lord that is involved in conversion to Christ. If we would receive the light of the New Covenant, we need to have the veil removed, and this only happens when we turn to the Lord.

Notice that both in verses 14 and 16, the veil is said to be 'taken away', so that, although in the Old Testament story it is Moses who removes it, in the New Testament parallel it is clearly God who takes it away.

The New Covenant is essentially a covenant of Divine action from start to finish, for the self-saving activity which was sinful man's response to the Old Covenant has been set aside and done away with. In the New Covenant, God himself writes his Law in our hearts (Jer. 31:31-34), for it is only through his work within us that we can obey it from the heart.

Verse 17 is not an easy verse, and we are surely right in seeking an understanding of it in terms of this Old Testament background story. Paul seems to be saying that the parallel to the Lord in the Old Covenant is the Spirit in the New. In what way can this be?

It is clear enough that, whatever it means, it implies the deity of the Holy Spirit. If he can be so equated with God, even though it is more in terms of his work than his Person, he is fully divine.

Because in this passage Paul has been writing more in terms of the inner work of the Spirit than of the atoning work of Christ (both of which are, of course, necessary), it is apt that he should carry this right through and see conversion as turning to the Spirit, that is, recognising the need for inner and transforming Divine power rather than self-effort.

There is also an interesting paradox here. If 'the Lord' in the Exodus passage really is equivalent to 'the Spirit' in the experience of Christian conversion, this implies that the Spirit has authority over us. Why? Because, the word 'Lord' particularly emphasizes the *authority* of God. Paradoxically, though, this 'Lord' gives freedom, for the Spirit brings us liberty when he frees us from the condemning, death-dealing effects of trying to find salvation through Law-keeping. Not only here but also in Romans 8:2, Paul relates Christian freedom to the inner work of the Spirit.

Verse 18 virtually sums up the positive content of all Paul has said since verse 6, while adding further important thoughts.

Through the inner work of the Spirit, Christians have the blinding veil removed from their faces. In the context here, this might appear to apply particularly to Hebrew Christians, although the opening verses of the next chapter tend to widen the application of the veil analogy.

Within the present context, 'we .... all' will imply a contrast with the situation in Moses' day. It was only he who stood in God's presence and received the imprint of the divine radiance on his countenance. The Old Covenant was made with Israel as a group through him as its mediator. In the New Covenant, however, although the group, the church, does not lack importance, the relationship offered gives inner knowledge of God to the individual believer (cf. Jer. 31:33,34). In a sense, then, we all go up the mountain. This is a wider privilege than obtained even in the ministry of Christ, when only three of the Twelve ascended the Transfiguration Mount with him (Luke 9:28).

The word translated 'reflect' is an interesting one and has two possible meanings. It can signify either looking or reflecting. The context makes it quite difficult to decide between these two meanings for either of them would fit well.

Could Paul in fact have been led to this word simply because of its ambiguity, and because it is true in this passage in both senses? There are other passages where he seems to use a word or phrase with two senses, both perfectly appropriate to the context, and this phenomenon is found more in this epistle than anywhere else in his writings.[1]

So then, we reflect by looking, just as Moses did. He could only see God's 'back parts' (Exod. 33:23) interpreted in the Exodus account as his goodness and his glory (Exod. 33:19-22). In the gospel however we are able to look into the glorious face of Christ (cf. 4:6). Although we may not see him with our physical eyes, as Paul did, the essence of that encounter is ours

---

1. See Introduction, p. 23.

inwardly, as the Lord who is the Spirit directs us to Christ.

The glory of the Lord (as Paul will make clear later in 4:4-6) is the glory of Christ, and it is to him, of course, that 'the Lord, who is the Spirit', directs us. The result of such looking and reflecting is Christlikeness, with perhaps a suggestion that this is the restoration of the moral image of God ('his likeness') in those who so look and reflect that glory.

Here then 'glorification' is not applied, as it so often is in Systematic Theology, to the consummation of God's work of salvation in us at Christ's return, but rather is an ongoing work within us, which Systematic Theology normally designates as 'sanctification'.

One last point: under the Old Covenant the glory, which was very real, was nevertheless a fading glory, for it was destined to fade away once the New Covenant had come, just as the glory of the moon is put 'in the shade' when the sun rises. As we have seen, this was symbolised by the fading of the glory on the face of Moses under the veil.

In the New Covenant, however, the glory does not fade but rather increases. If we do look constantly into the face of Christ, we will reflect his character more and more.

There is no other way to be like Christ!

Some questions for personal reflection:

1. How can I use the Old Testament to show from its pages the great glory of Christ?

2. Is it important for us to witness to Jews today about Jesus as the Messiah?

3. Have I realized the extent of Christ's concern to transform my life and the lives of others and make us like him?

4. Am I reflecting? Am I looking?

6: SINCERE BUT FRAIL (4:1-12)

Even the most cursory glance makes it clear to the reader that this section of Paul's letter is closely connected to the last. The ideas of glory, ministry and veiling, which were so important in chapter 3, reappear here.

These verses are very encouraging, and may well represent the kind of thoughts that encouraged the apostle himself in his work for the Lord. They will help us too, for there are times when we all need some encouragement.

1. Clear truth from sincere hearts (4:1-4)

The gospel of the New Covenant has wonderful power to transform the characters of those who receive it (3:2,3), for it brings us into fellowship with Christ, whose character we may reflect as we look at him (3:18). This may well be why Paul says that he does not lose heart. Problems he undoubtedly has, but while God is changing the characters and conduct of men and women through his ministry he will not lose heart.

The ministry he and his companions have is in fact a product of the mercy of God. This shows that he regarded preaching the gospel as a great privilege conferred on him by God. In Ephesians 3:7,8, he makes the same point, although there he employs the word 'grace' instead of 'mercy'. It is important for us to remember that it is not only salvation that is given to us apart from our deserts, but service also. This means that there can be no pride of status in any position we may hold in Christian work.

In verse 2, there are three related disclaimers. The fact that he uses the language of commendation again (cf. 3:1) shows that he is very much aware of facing criticism.

In saying that he has 'renounced secret and shameful ways' and that he does not 'use deception', Paul is probably referring to the accusations some were bringing against him at Corinth. He had said he would come to them, but had not arrived (in fact, for very good reasons: 1:23-2:4), and this was taken by some there as a symptom of his little concern for the truth.

Paul has of course rebutted this charge already. In fact it was one of his first concerns in this letter to do just that (1:12-2:4). Acceptance of the truthfulness of the gospel is often tied to the known integrity or otherwise of the messengers themselves. He has already said that his 'Yes' is 'Yes' and his 'No,' 'No' (1:17-20), and also that the message of Christ is not both 'Yes' and 'No' at once.

If Judaizing influences were present at Corinth,[1] Paul may also have been accused of distorting the word of God. This is because the Judaizers held that the Gentiles ought to be brought under the Law and receive circumcision as a sign of the covenant just like the Jews, and Paul was opposed to this, as Acts 15:1,2 and his Epistle to the Galatians show us.

Giving out the gospel plainly and clearly in all its truth is not undertaken for personal ends, but rather for the glory of God in the salvation of men and women. It is evident, however, from what Paul says here, that he saw it can also be a testimony to the integrity of the person who communicates it. He is not of course laying stress on the intellectual clarity which is involved in clear communication, important as this may be, but on the fact that the preacher must be absolutely straight with his hearers. It is the plain truth he must tell.

So behind what he is saying is the important principle that message and messenger are mutually vindicating. How deeply challenging for any today who are called to preach the good news of Christ!

Incidentally we note that Paul here describes the gospel as 'the truth'. This is not a popular idea today, for there is wide-

---

1. See Introduction, p. 15.

spread belief in the relativity of truth. It is often said that what is true for me may not be true for you, with the implication that we should be infinitely tolerant and not seek to persuade others to change their beliefs. Paul clearly held that there was such a thing as the absolute truth, and that this was in fact the gospel of Christ.

Although he says that this commendation is to the conscience it is also in the sight of God, for Paul recognised that the final arbiter of truth could never be in the human heart but can only be God himself.

The truth is set forth plainly and yet we have to reckon with the fact that it is not always understood (4:3,4). There were many who did not understand our Lord during the days of his ministry (e.g. see John 6:41-66). Just as the Law could be veiled because of the spiritual dullness of those to whom it was addressed (3:13-16), so also can the gospel be. This is, in other words, something common to the contents of both testaments. Both present truth, but both can be misunderstood.

'And even if our gospel is veiled' – why 'even'? Because it might seem strange to the readers that, with the coming of the New Covenant, there should be any veiling. They might well have thought this to be a condition only of the Old Covenant and not of the new.

Paul recognized that this was not so, but that in every age Satan is at work in seeking to blind people to truth. We need to remember this today. Not only should the Word be preached, but there needs to be prayer too, because constant and total dependence on God to reveal his truth and to open blinded eyes is quite indispensable.

To whom is Paul referring when he writes of 'those who are perishing'? Clearly we cannot restrict this description either to Jews or Gentiles, for Paul preached the gospel message to both, and in each case there was need for repentance and faith in Christ.

What precisely does he mean by 'perishing'? There are two main views. One is that extermination is in view, complete annihilation of the total man, while the other, more traditional, view is that it is eternal punishment. Certainly the former would be possible within the Greek word's range of meanings, but we should note that it is used of Judas by our Lord in John 17:12 and that the same man is said by Peter in Acts 1:25 to have gone 'where he belongs,' which hardly suggests annihilation.

Paul uses the same word in 1 Corinthians 1:18. The tense is present continuous in both places. This suggests a process which begins in this life and we might compare with this the statements of Christ that the one who does not believe 'stands condemned already' (John 3:18) and that, as far as someone who rejects the Son is concerned, 'the wrath of God remains on him' (John 3:36).

'The god of this age' is a startling and unique expression, although it may remind us of Christ's own description of Satan as 'the prince of this world' (John 12:31). Paul writes of 'this present evil age' (Gal. 1:4) and John says that 'the whole world is under the control of the evil one' (1 John 5:19).

Why 'god'? Because of the power he exercises, and also because worship is directed to him. If Paul can say that 'the sacrifices of pagans are offered to demons, not to God' (1 Cor. 10:20), this must also be true of Satan, their leader. You do not have to be a Satanist to worship the devil, but simply choose any false object of worship.

Here Paul writes about a blindness of the mind just as in 3:14 he says, 'their minds were made dull.' It is much the same thought, for both expressions suggest a lack of response to stimulus, from the light or from the truth.

Somebody has well said, 'Cameras and eyes are blind; it is only minds that see.' It is not the instrument of sight, whether mechanical or fleshly, that discerns meaning. Your camera or your eye may register what is there but be quite unable to interpret it.

How sad then when the mind, given to us for understanding what we see, hear or touch, is itself blind, deaf or insensitive! Also we may see and understand the physical world and yet be quite blind to spiritual realities. It is this kind of blindness that Satan has so effectively secured.

It is then Satan who does this, but it is also the operation of a Divine law, for, in the realm of spiritual insight, God has joined faith and insight and also unbelief and blindness. Satan has a ready-made instrument for his schemes in the unbelief of men and women. In spiritual things, it is not really true that seeing is believing; it would be much nearer the mark to say that believing is seeing.

The wonderful expression, 'the light of the gospel of the glory of Christ, who is the image of God', is best tackled from back to front.

'The image of God' reminds us of Genesis 1:26,27. It is possible that Paul knew the thought of Philo, the Alexandrian Jew who was his older contemporary. Philo was very much influenced by the philosophy of Plato, the Greek, who taught that earthly things, which are imperfect, have their perfect counterparts in another world. In line with this, Philo taught that when God made man on earth in his own image, he also made a perfect image of himself in the heavenly realms.

Now this is not Biblical, and yet for Paul there is an element of truth in it, for there is a perfect image of God, although not one that was created, for he is in fact the eternal Christ. We find this thought also in Colossians 1:15; John 1:18, and Hebrews 1:3, although a different Greek word is used in the last of these.

When Christ came to earth, the grace and truth that characterized him revealed the character of God (John 1:14-18). A special occasion like the Transfiguration simply meant that a glory then radiated from his body which matched and expressed the inward spiritual glory that was always his, the Divine glory proper to him (Luke 9:28ff.).

So Christ's revelation of God is wonderfully good news, for it shows that God cares for his imperfect world, for men and women in whom his image is so sadly marred as to be at times almost unrecognisable.

2. Glorious light from clay lamps (4:5-7)

Paul has had to engage in some self-vindication for the sake of the gospel (1:12-2:4; 2:17-3:6; 4:1-3), but when he actually preaches the good news he does not talk about himself (v.5). He preaches Jesus Christ as Lord. Like John the Baptist (John 1:19-37; 3:26-30), he points away from himself to Christ.

His message contains clear reference to the transcendence of Christ, to his Lordship, his deity. The Lordship of Christ and his standing as God's Son were of course singularly attested by God when he raised him from the dead (Rom. 1:4; 10:9).

If the preacher is asked, of course, he confesses himself to be a servant (literally 'a slave') of others for Christ's sake. This is an unexpected thought. To reckon himself a slave of Christ was part of Paul's regular outlook (Rom. 1:1; Phil. 1:1; Titus 1:1), as it was that of other New Testament writers (James 1:1; 2 Pet. 1:1; Jude 1), but it was quite something else to confess himself a slave of others. The words, 'for Christ's sake' are therefore of crucial importance.

A man may have a slave. Another man visits him and he wants to honour him and assist him. He therefore makes his slave available to him to care for his needs. This slave belongs to the first man, not the second, but he serves the first by serving the second.

To take such a lowly place needs grace, but it is following the Master, who took the place of a slave to his Father (Phil.

2:7) and as such a slave, served sinners for his Father by dying for them. In his Letter to the Romans, written not long after 2 Corinthians, he exhorted them to accept one another, and pointed to the example of Christ, who served both Jew and Gentile on behalf of God's truth (Rom. 15:7-9).

Although Paul uses the first person plural in verse 6, there can be little doubt that he is thinking chiefly about his own conversion. He has been thinking about the glory of Christ and also about the privilege of preaching the good news. Now in fact it was from the glorified and therefore glorious Christ that he had gone out to proclaim the gospel. He can vividly recall it all when he stands in imagination once again on that unforgettable road to Damascus. See also our comment on 5:16-18a.

Paul's conversion experience is recorded no less than three times in Acts, once by Luke in his narrative (Acts 9) and twice by Paul as he recalls it all on two later occasions (Acts 22, 26). It would be worth reading these accounts at this point.

How could Paul explain to his readers what that experience was like? Undoubtedly it was an experience of light, for Christ appeared to him in glorious light and a flood of light shone on his path. But this light was not simply an external phenomenon. It entered into his very heart. As he said to the Galatians, 'God ... was pleased to reveal his Son in me' (Gal. 1:16). Notice that he says 'in me', not 'to me'. Quite literally it is 'into me', a most apt phrase for a revelation that came from an external Source but flooded his heart with light.

He saw 'the light of the knowledge of the glory of God in the face of Christ'. 'Face' is a word that arrests the reader's attention and it may well have two senses, both of them intended by Paul.[2]

Paul saw the glory of God quite literally in the face of Christ, for he saw the glorified Christ with his actual physical eyes. No

---

2. See Introduction, p. 23.

doubt he would never forget that Face.

Then 'face' had come also to mean 'person'. When we think of another person it is normally that person's face that comes before us through our imaginative faculty. It is in the face that the person finds expression. The term 'face' is even used of God in the Old Testament, when God says that nobody can see his Face (Exod. 33:20). This is tantamount to saying that the revelation he gives of himself is only partial.

Paul saw the face of Christ in the sense that he saw Christ as a Person, and he saw God revealed in him. So light came to him, not simply in the sense that it shone into his dark, rebellious heart, but also that, when this happened, it gave him true knowledge of God.

So, for him, everything started with that great encounter with Christ, everything went back to that encounter. There his thought took its rise as from its spring, and returned to it as its ocean.

To what then could such an experience be compared? In an analogy that fairly takes our breath away, Paul compares it to the first day of creation, when God said, 'Let there be light'. What an incredible claim! But conversion really is that, for the new birth is at the same time a new creation. It is our introduction to a new world, a new heaven and earth that will be consummated at the climax of God's programme of redemptive action for this world of his (Rev. 21:1ff.). Paul takes up this new creation theme again later (5:16-18).

Such a great revelation could perhaps make a man or woman arrogant, although it should have no such effect. Later Paul writes about some subsequent revelations God gave to him and of the way God sought to keep him humble (12:1-10). Here (v. 7) Paul sees that pride is totally inappropriate, for he realises how humble is the vessel in which such a revelation is contained. It is simply a clay jar.

What does he intend by this analogy? He writes of treasure,

and so he is often thought to have the normal 'banking' arrangements of the day in mind. People with precious treasures who were anxious about thieves usually hid them in the commonest, cheapest pots they could find, provided they did not easily break, in the hope that thieves would overlook them.

On the other hand, it is possible, especially in view of the context, that he had in mind the clay lamps that could be bought in any marketplace. Did he perhaps know of the two sayings of our Lord, 'I am the light of the world' (John 8:12), and 'You are the light of the world' (Matt. 5:14)? Without doubt, his thought here would perfectly illustrate the connection we may discern between these two sayings. It is the indwelling Christ who makes us the light of the world, for the light we transmit is not our own but his.

Which interpretation are we to take? As we have suggested earlier[3] it may well be that Paul had both ideas in mind, and that the use of the word 'treasure' instead of 'light' may have been determined by a kind of creative ambiguity. We do have great treasure in our hearts, the treasure of the gospel, but this treasure is also light, which is to shine out through us. As Paul makes it clear, we are not the originators of this treasure/light but simply its communicators.

He writes of 'all-surpassing power', in a phrase that may remind us of the Letter to the Ephesians, with its many superlatives and similar expressions underlining the greatness of the gospel of Christ.

3. Abundant life from dying men (4:8-12)
These verses are in a sense a development of verse 7, as the translators of the NIV have perhaps noted by the way they have paragraphed this part of the letter. The 'jars of clay' are subject to a great deal of pressure of various kinds.

---

3. See Introduction, p. 23.

This is first stated generally in the words 'hard pressed on every side, but not crushed' (v.8). Paul's language here perhaps reflects the analogy with the jars. Although subject to pressure, they are still intact, so that they can still contain the treasure, still transmit the light.

Christians do not always understand the ways of God, they can be perplexed, but, because of faith, this does not lead to despair. They are confident that there is in the dealings of God with them a reason known to him, and they are willing to await the disclosure of that later.

They may face persecution, for their faith challenges the unbeliever and may well rouse him to violent opposition. In this they experience love of God which never lets them go, as Paul says so eloquently in Romans 8:31-39.

'Struck down, but not destroyed' or, as Moffatt puts it, using the language of the boxing ring, 'knocked down but not knocked out', which does in fact express the essence of the thought quite well. Their buffetings do not make them give up but simply cause them to look for grace to persist.

Verse 10 introduces a new note. Paul had a deep awareness of union with Christ, and as Romans 6, written only shortly after this letter, makes clear, this union was with the Christ who died and rose again. Because of this there is a communication to the believer of these two experiences of Christ. He knows a 'death' as well as a 'resurrection', for in willing submission to the death of his own plans he finds newness of life.

It is interesting here that Paul does not actually say that we carry around in our bodies the death of Jesus, but rather (for this is the literal meaning) the dying of Jesus. Here the AV is much better than the NIV.

This distinction is no subtlety. So often Christians say they have no fear of death but only of dying. Dying can be painful, prolonged and puzzling. For us death is glorious although dying may still be painful. Even for our Lord, death took place in a moment, the moment when he dismissed his spirit, but all the way to Jerusalem, in Gethsemane, in the judgment hall, amid the mockery and shame and hanging on the cross itself Jesus was dying.

Verses 10 and 11 express exactly the same thought in different words. Why? Perhaps the repetition is because the idea may have been new to the Corinthians, and because spiritually it is so challenging and at the same time so encouraging.

The encouragement comes clearly in verse 12. What is the apostle saying here? He is explaining to his readers that his dying, and the dying of his fellow-workers, means life, not only for them, but also for the Corinthian believers they are serving with and in the gospel. It is not just life for ourselves that we discover to be at work when we accept dying, but life for others.

There can, in other words, be no fruitfulness in service for Christ until we are prepared to die. It was the way the Master went, should not the servant tread it still?

Some questions for personal reflection:

1. In what ways can the Word of God be distorted in our communication of it today?

2. When we encounter much spiritual blindness on the part of our hearers, what should we do?

3. How can we highlight the glory of Christ so that people become aware of his greatness and grace?

4. What, in practical terms, do I know about carrying around in my body the dying of Jesus?

7: WAITING FOR A BETTER HOME (4:13-5:10)

Most of us could do with more patience.

When we are babies, we cry if the milk is withdrawn from us even for a few seconds. When we are children, we live in anticipation of special dates. There are our birthdays and Christmas, and the start of the school holidays. Always we are looking forward to something, and longing for it to get here sooner than we know it really will.

Do we lose this as adults? Not altogether. It may be that experience has taught us we should not count our chickens before they are hatched and that hope sometimes has to be deferred. Yet we don't altogether lose the impatience of children.

As Christians, there is no doubt where our hope lies. It is the return of Christ, for it is his coming that will issue in the climax of God's great purpose which his Word has promised and which we so eagerly expect – or do we?

Some of us have become just a little too patient. The eager cry of the Book of the Revelation, 'Come, Lord Jesus!' (Rev. 22:20), finds but a dull echo in our hearts. We make a somewhat formal acknowledgement of the fact that the present world order is to come to an end when Jesus returns, and then settle down once more to our life in this materialistic society.

Paul's own attitude was just about right. He knew that Christ was to return, and he longed for that, but he knew too that this same Christ had commissioned him to preach the gospel. In fact, as we shall see, he found encouragement from his future hope to help him in his present work.

1. Encouragement to proclaim the gospel (4:13-15)

Paul has been thinking about death and life as two principles at work in his present life as a Christian (4:10-12) and he has used the phrase 'our mortal body' (v. 11). So often a phrase seems to stimulate further thoughts in his mind and this has certainly happened here, for he now begins to dwell on the future and how God is going to transform this mortal body.

His quotation from Psalm 116:10 here (v. 13) is most interesting and instructive. The psalm is a hymn of praise occasioned by the psalmist's deliverance from death. What is particularly interesting is the fact that his assertion of faith comes in a part of the psalm where he is describing his experience of distress and also his disillusionment with people. Here then faith was under real pressure from circumstances and yet was exercised in a most positive way.

How appropriate then in application to the circumstances of Paul's own life as described in verses 7 to 12! Perhaps this reflects something of his devotional life, and we wonder if he had been reading this psalm in the midst of his own experiences of trial.

Let us note also that he goes on to say, 'With that same spirit of faith...' Most of our translations use a lower case letter for the 's' of 'spirit', but this should not hide from us the fact that such a spirit, such a disposition, is due to the work of the Spirit of God within the heart.

Here then Paul senses that he and David have spiritual kinship, and he recognizes that the same Spirit is at work within people of the Old and New covenants. This is interesting, for it shows that the contrast between the two covenants which he outlined so eloquently in chapter 3 is relative rather than absolute.

It is interesting that Paul links faith and speech here, for he does this also in Romans 10:9,10. It is out of the fulness of the heart that the mouth speaks, and genuine faith should certainly find expression in our verbal witness.

That witness is, of course, both in Romans 10 and here (v. 14), to the crucified and risen Christ, who is the very heart of the gospel.

It is worth noting that in the New Testament the resurrection of Jesus is more often related to the power of the Father than to that of the Son, although references to the latter are not altogether absent (e.g. John 10:17,18). The importance of this great act by the Father is that it took place as vindication of his Son, so Peter, preaching in Jerusalem, the very place where it all happened, says, 'You .... put him to death by nailing him to the cross, but God raised him from the dead .... because it was impossible for death to keep its hold on him' (Acts 2:23,24).

Paul has already made reference to the spiritual resurrection of believers (vv. 10, 11), but now he asserts his belief also in their bodily resurrection. In fact, the one is really an earnest, a pledge and foretaste, of the other. It is not surprising that he links the resurrection of Christ and that of believers so intimately here, for, the Corinthians would recall, he did exactly this in 1 Corinthians 15.

The fellowship between the evangelists and those they had been privileged to reach for Christ would go on beyond the Second Advent, for they would have the joy of being together in the presence of Christ (v. 14). Elsewhere (e.g. 1 Thess. 2:19, 20) Paul refers to his anticipation of great joy in seeing those he has led to Christ also glorified when Christ comes again.

Here he says that God will 'raise us with Jesus and present us with you in his presence'. Does he mean the presence of God or of Christ?

There may be a clue in the verb *paristemi*, translated 'present'. It is also used in 11:2, where Paul writes of presenting the church as a pure virgin to Christ, viewing himself, of course, as an instrument of God in his ministry to the church. It occurs also in Ephesians 5:27 where it is Christ who presents the church, holy and blameless, to himself.

Certainly Paul makes no express reference here to the church as Christ's bride, but his use of this verb may suggest he already has the thought in his mind. In that case, 'in his presence' will refer to Christ, to whom the church is to be presented.

Perhaps one of the most trying aspects of suffering lies in the fact that it sometimes seems to us to be without purpose, although often, if we pray for discernment, God will show us something of its meaning. Paul's own words, 'with you' (v. 14), remind him that there is a purpose in his sufferings, a purpose for the Corinthians themselves (v. 15; cf. 1:6). He is prepared to endure suffering for their sakes. He is being enabled in the context of suffering to reach more and more people with the message of the grace of God.

As a result of this there is a great overflow of praise from many hearts (cf. 1:10). There is nothing that so moves our hearts to praise God as the knowledge that he has saved us by his grace.

Here then we can see clearly that the ultimate motive of Paul's work is not found amongst men, not even in their salvation, but in God himself. He wants to see God glorified.

2. Encouragement to look to the unseen (4:16-18)

To find God so honouring his work, even through suffering, is a real encouragement to him. The sufferings are real but he is not preoccupied with them. Rather he keeps his eye on those great ends God is bringing about through them.

In verses 16 to 18, he operates with two pairs of antitheses, the outward and the inward, the temporary and the eternal, and it is most instructive to see how he does this.

Verse 16 perhaps takes up the implied contrast of the inner and the outer that we find in verses 10 to 14, for there he begins with spiritual resurrection and moves on to physical. Already he and his fellow-believers are experiencing the spiritual resurrection, but the physical is yet to come.

Paul's body may not look at the moment as if it has an eternal destiny. It is, he says 'wasting away', perhaps a summary of what he says in verses 9 and 10. As we read the long catalogue of his sufferings given in 11:23-27, we can have little doubt that he will have suffered physically from the many afflictions he had endured. For one thing he probably bore still the marks of what he had endured at the hands of his persecutors.

There is however an inward renewal and this is going on all the time. Roy Clements says, 'I don't care how old you are or how weak you feel; if you are a Christian then the resurrection life of Jesus is glowing inside you like an atomic pile, radiating the energy of the world to come.'[1] Perhaps Paul's reference to the Old Testament a few verses back (v. 13) gives us a clue to an important channel of that inward renewal. God's Spirit would use the Old Testament Scriptures daily to encourage him in the gospel task he had been given. He still uses these Scriptures to this end.

Verse 17 is astonishing, even in the context of verses 8 to 12, and even more when what he says in chapter 11 is borne in mind. Whatever may be said about his sufferings they seem anything but 'light and momentary troubles'. A lot depends, of course, on our standards of measurement and on what our real scale of values is.

Here Paul may be playing on the original meaning of the Hebrew *kabod*, which is rendered into Greek by *doxa* ('glory'), on which we commented earlier (see on 3:14-18). From the eternal perspective, glory is substantial and sufferings are light-weight. The expression, 'far outweighs' is a very strong one in

1. *The Strength of Weakness*, p. 96.

the Greek. It is almost as if Paul is saying that to compare the two is ridiculous. It is certainly a greatly encouraging thought. In his book *The Great Divorce*, C. S. Lewis takes up the idea and he represents the heavenly realm as far more substantial than the earthly.

Paul does not however simply contrast the sufferings and the glory; he connects them, for the one is a means to the other. The same thought, differently expressed, also occurs in Romans 8:17.

What does this imply? Probably that the pattern of sufferings followed by glory, established by Christ himself in his own life, is God's own pattern for his people, and that we should not seek to escape from it but rather to accept it as God's will for us. In some way, either as reward or else as a result of the moulding of character that patient endurance of suffering brings, future glory will have been effected by God through that suffering.

In verse 18 Paul brings together both antitheses into one verse, and in so doing he identifies the seen with the temporary and the unseen with the eternal.

We should not miss the place this verse gives to fixing our eyes on the unseen, the eternal. The NIV does not bring out the fact that verses 17 and 18 are tied together grammatically, for Paul is saying that 'our light and momentary troubles are achieving for us an eternal weight of glory that far outweighs them all, as [or 'while' or even 'providing'] we fix our eyes ....' So the seeing is a means to an end.

It is most interesting to compare this with 3:18, where Paul sees that our progressive transformation into the likeness of Christ is brought about as we look at him and reflect his glory. The difference between the two verses is that while in both Paul is thinking of the importance of looking at Christ or at eternal things, there his emphasis is on the results of this in this life while here it is on the results for the life to come.

3. Encouragement to hope for the future (5:1-5)

These verses are not without problems, and they have been interpreted in more than one way.

We notice first of all that Paul is operating here with two metaphors, the tent replaced by the house, and unclothing and clothing. We should also notice that he uses another more literal antithesis, that between mortality and life. He then says that the Spirit is the guarantee of the change.

The main issue is whether he is thinking of the fact that we have an abode in heaven or of our heavenly body.

The tent/house antithesis certainly suggests the former, perhaps with the kind of teaching given in John 14:2 in view. We now live in temporary quarters, with no enduring city (Heb. 13:14), a kind of nomadic existence, although we are longing for a more permanent abode and God will one day give us this. The metaphor of tent-dwelling, the lifestyle of the nomad, is well fitted to picture this.

In addition to this, we notice that this house is said to be 'not built by human hands' (v. 1), and the false witnesses at the trial of Jesus said that he had threatened to destroy the temple made by human hands, which is the literal meaning of their words in Mark 14:58.

This last argument is, however, double-edged, for in fact the words of the false witnesses were a misinterpretation of a saying of our Lord which he himself intended to refer to his body (John 2:19-21). So we have a precedent in the teaching of Jesus for an analogy between a building (in his case, a temple) and a body. So the house not made with human hands could be the resurrection body, for this would fit exactly with what our Lord said in John 2.

The unclothing/clothing figure too is much more suggestive of the body, for Paul uses this metaphor in other places for our commitment as Christians to a new lifestyle, the lifestyle of

Christ (e.g. Rom. 13:12-14; Eph. 4:22-24). Such language then would be altogether appropriate for the consummation of our new existence in the resurrection, especially as Paul has already been operating with the thought of a spiritual followed by a physical resurrection (4:10-14).

In addition to this, the groaning of the Christian (vv. 2,4) is referred to also in Romans 8:23 and it is due to our eager desire for the redemption of our bodies.

Note the great assurance of the present tense, 'we have'. Through Christ, it is ours as surely as if it had already come into our experience.

Why does he mention our desire not to be unclothed (v. 4)? It is difficult to make sense of this if he is thinking in terms of earthly and heavenly dwellings, but if it is the body that is in view, it would make sense. After all, the real hope of the Christian is not in the temporary separation of body and soul at death, but the glorious resurrection that lies beyond this. 'That what is mortal may be swallowed up by life' would itself give the Corinthian readers a clue to Paul's meaning, for he had used this sort of language, and in close connection with the metaphor of clothing, in his first letter to them (1 Cor. 15:53, 54).

The Spirit too is more appropriate as an earnest of our resurrection than as a guarantee of a home in God's presence, for his work now relates to our inward life, and this is a pledge of the fuller life of the resurrection that is to come. For the Greek word *arrabon* ('deposit') here see the comment on 1:22.

All in all, it seems most likely that it is the resurrection of the body that Paul has in mind throughout this passage, and that he has taken the building analogy from our Lord's own words as recorded in John 2.

4. Encouragement to please the Lord (5:6-10)

The two parts of the statement in verse 6 appear at first sight to be contradictory, but in fact they are not. Paul says that the ground of our confidence lies in the fact that one day we will be at home with the Lord.

By 'away from the Lord' he means, of course, away from his physical presence and one of the qualities of that presence is visibility, so that we must live by faith, not by sight (v. 7). He would not want his readers to think he was saying they had no real present experience of the Lord. It was a faith and not a sight experience, but none the less real for that.

His confidence in the future means he really lives in strong anticipation of what is to come. How does verse 8 square with verse 4? Is not death before the Lord's advent a kind of unclothing, even if it is to be present with the Lord? Perhaps so, but the main thing is the presence of the Lord and this is what really matters. Paul does not say anything about the intermediate state between death and resurrection, for his main thought is not about the person's state but about the wonder of being with Christ.

The Christian does not only live in anticipation of being with Christ, he is also encouraged to please him in everything (v. 9). To emphasise this, Paul points out that the Christian has a judgment to face (v. 10).

This too may appear to contradict Paul's teaching about the justification of the Christian believer by grace and his consequent freedom from condemnation (e.g. Romans 5:1; 8:1), but it does not. There is no reference here to condemnation, but there is a recognition of responsibility, of accountability.

There will be rewards but there will also be loss, although, as Paul has already taught his readers in 1 Corinthians 3:10-15, this loss will not mean a forfeiting of salvation.

Some questions for personal reflection:

1. In what ways have I been encouraged in my Christian life from the Old Testament?

2. What part does my future hope play in encouraging me to continue my work for the Lord?

3. How mindful am I of the fact that my work will be judged by the Lord?

8: OFFERING PEACE (5:11-6:2)

As we suggested in the Introduction,[1] this epistle gives us considerable insight into the mind and heart of the apostle Paul.

The Acts of the Apostles tells us many of the outward facts about his missionary vocation: where he went, how long he stayed, who he met, what he said, what God did through him and his friends. It also makes clear of course the crucial role of the Holy Spirit in his ministry, without whom nothing he did would have been effective for God.

In addition to this, we are made aware of his feelings from time to time. We see how deeply distressed he was that human beings should turn aside from the God who made them and worship instead what he has created (Acts 14:14 and 17:16). We see too the depth of his feelings for those he had led to Christ (Acts 20:19). Luke, always honest, shows us too that he could be sharp in his disagreement over a matter about which he felt strongly (Acts 14:39).

It is when we come to his letters, though, that we can see more deeply into his heart. This is especially true of this particular letter. Perhaps only 1 Thessalonians, a much shorter letter, comes near it as far as this is concerned.

The council of a missionary society or the ministerial recognition committee of a denomination is likely to ask questions, not simply about a candidate's experience in Christian work, but about what it is that makes that person 'tick' as a servant of Christ. It is important that they should, for it is what we are as Christians that matters most in our service. Paul gives us such a full and frank insight into his heart here that we are left in no doubt about the inner motives of his extensive and demanding missionary life.

1. See Introduction, pp. 17, 18.

1. His motivation and convictions (5:11-15)

Paul here refers to two motives we might have thought mutually exclusive. In verse 11, he writes of the fear of the Lord and in verse 14 of the love of Christ. Both of these exercise motivating power in his service for Christ.

But how can these two emotions or attitudes co-exist? In his First Epistle, John declares, 'There is no fear in love. But perfect love drives out fear, because fear has to do with punishment. The one who fears is not made perfect in love' (1 John 4:18).

In this kind of apparent contradiction, we usually find that a word or phrase is used in two different senses, so that the conflict is more apparent than real. The fear mentioned in our passage is an attitude towards the very same Lord Paul says will provide us with our heavenly dwelling and with whom he longs to be, as verses 1 to 8 make clear to us. We can hardly think that he will, on the one hand, provide us with a heavenly dwelling, and on the other will send us to hell! That's not merely an apparent contradiction, but utter nonsense!

Moreover, these verses were certainly not written by a man who feared God's awful sentence of condemnation, although, as we see in verses 9 and 10, by somebody who wanted to please the Lord in view of the judgment he would face as a believer.

So then this fear must be a different type from what John has in mind. It is a reverential awe, the feeling you would have towards somebody you both love and respect, and to whom you are accountable. In fact it suggests the kind of attitude a child would have to his or her father within a good family relationship. In such a situation, it is not so much a child's fear of punishment that is the dominant emotion, but a fear of hurting somebody he or she loves.

Living for Christ is a serious commitment to our heavenly Father's plan for us, and one day its quality will be assessed by him. This is why Paul engages in the task of persuasion which was God's will for him.

Persuasion implies using truth to move the will, and this is what real Christian preaching is. True preaching does not try to bombard the will by stirring emotion through psychological techniques. Instead it presents compelling truth and convincing arguments. This does not mean there will be no emotional content to gospel preaching, but that this will arise from its essential message and not be artificially attached to it. It is truth that moves us most deeply to action, and depth is of supreme importance here.

When is truth most persuasive? When it is illustrated in the lives of those who proclaim it. In view of this, we can understand why Paul once again takes up the matter of his sincerity (cf. 1:12ff.; 4:1ff.); The whole point of this, as he makes clear (v. 12), is not to establish the messengers as paragons of virtue, but rather to undergird the credibility of the message by the credibility of its human vehicles.

Paul's critics at Corinth were superficial in their judgments. They looked at the outward appearance (cf. 1 Sam. 16:7). Very well, those who thoroughly accept Paul's integrity have answers to their criticisms, and Paul's point is that to give these answers will actually support not only the messenger, but also the message.

What does verse 13 mean? There is no agreed answer and the larger commentaries usually give a survey of different interpretations.

It is fairly obvious that Paul is still thinking of his critics at Corinth. For some reason or other, they had accused him of being mentally unbalanced. What he is saying then is that his true motives are for the glory of God and for the salvation of people. If that is labelled 'mad', perhaps the critics should look again at the criteria they use for judging madness and sanity.

One man's madness may be another man's soundness of mind, and this is because the wisdom of God cuts right across human wisdom (cf. 1 Cor. 1:18-25).

In fact, Paul is motivated by the love of Christ (v. 14). What does he mean by this expression, Christ's love for him or his love for Christ? Either is a possible way of understanding the phrase he uses (cf. Rom. 5:5). This may be studied ambiguity so that we will not need to choose between the two.[2]

We may argue from the parallel with 'the fear of the Lord' that it is our love for Christ (see. v. 11 and the comment there). On the other hand, the words in 14b and 15 that follow his reference to the love of Christ are really all about Christ's love for us, so that this is what we should probably emphasize. It is Christ's love for us that evokes from us a responsive love (1 John 4:19), and that love, as again John shows very clearly in 1 John 3:16-18, reveals itself unambiguously when it constrains us to love others.

Paul's 'fear' (v. 11) was occasioned by something that is to occur in the future, the judgment seat of Christ, but his love is drawn out by something that had occurred in the past, the cross of Christ. This provided Paul and his friends with a very deep motive for their work, the motive of overflowing gratitude.

'We are convinced', he says. This is not simply an historical conviction, that is, an assurance that Christ died, but a theological one, 'that one died for all'. We are not commissioned simply to preach an event in history, but to declare the wonderful meaning that God himself attaches to that event.

The cross means substitution. Christ takes our place, bearing our punishment, as Paul makes so clear in verse 21. So the death of One was the death of all, for he took their place. His death was reckoned to be theirs.

Because they died, not literally but in a substitute, they have

2. See Introduction, p. 23.

life still, but the death of Christ makes all the difference in the world to the style of that life, for they now feel deep gratitude towards him, so that they want to live for him.

The One for whom they are now living is described as 'him who died for them and was raised again'. Paul is reminding his readers that God had shown his acceptance of Christ's death as a sacrifice for sins by raising him out of death. There can be no question of their living for a disgraced Messianic claimant, but rather for One vouched for by God himself (cf. Acts 13:27-31; Rom. 1:4; 4:25).

2. His outlook and re-creation (5:16-18a)

How radically our viewpoint changes when we are converted to Christ and begin to see what he has done for us on the cross! It revolutionizes our whole outlook, and especially the way we look at people.

What is it to regard somebody from a worldly point of view? It may take a number of different forms. I may perhaps think about that person in terms of his or her status or bank balance or gifts or personality. I may also, of course, view him or her as a means to an end, somebody to be exploited for my own pleasure or gain or self-esteem.

Unhappily, this kind of attitude is not dead even among Christians. Why is this? Could it be, as this passage may well suggest to us, that we do not spend enough time at the cross, and so are not as fully motivated by love for Christ as we ought to be?

Paul then goes on to make a statement that has caused a lot of debate, much of it quite unnecessary. 'From a worldly point of view' is literally 'according to the flesh', and Paul uses this expression both of people generally and of Christ in particular in verse 16.

Some writers have taken this to mean, 'as he was in the days of his flesh'. So, at this point, there has been discussion as to

whether Paul ever encountered Jesus during his earthly ministry, and even whether, after grasping the fact of the resurrection, he had any interest still in that earthly life.

All this is quite beside the point, as a study of the context
shows. 'According to the flesh' must mean the same here both
in application to people and in application to Christ. It can therefore hardly have any other sense than 'from a worldly point of
view'.

So then Paul is saying that he had entirely misjudged Jesus
prior to his conversion. His use of the word 'Christ' for him
here is significant, because, of course, when given its precise
meaning, it is the Greek equivalent of the Hebrew, 'Messiah',
which refers to the great Anointed One God was to send to save
his people.

There can be no doubt at all that before his conversion Paul
would never have accepted the idea that somebody who claimed
to be the Messiah was really what he claimed to be if that person had been crucified, for he would have taken it that this meant
God had rejected him, especially in the light of Deuteronomy
21:22,23. Now though he can see clearly that this death was
endured by Christ for others and not for himself, for it was the
bearing of God's penalty for sins. Christ could not have died
because of his own sins, for he had none. Notice how Paul interprets the Deuteronomy passage in Galatians 3:13,14.

We might compare here what happened in Peter's life and
how his outlook too changed radically. He had confessed Jesus
as the Christ but could not accept his statement that he would
be crucified (Mark 8:29-33). In his first letter, however, he constantly uses the word 'Christ' in close connection with references to the death of Jesus (1 Peter 1:11; 2:21; 3:18; 4:1; 5:1).
Could he have shown us more clearly what a change of outlook
he had experienced?

In this way, the cross, the very cause of difficulty both for

Paul and Peter, became the heart of their faith in Jesus as the Christ.

To be a Christian was, for Paul, to be 'in Christ' (see especially Eph. 1:3-14), in vital spiritual union with him. To be so united to him is to be a new creation (Eph. 2:10). God's great promise of a new world (Isa. 65:17; 66:22) has found fulfilment already in the new creation of people who will one day occupy that new world (cf. Rom. 8:18-21). The cross as preached to us in the message and the Holy Spirit effecting the new creation within our hearts – it is these that have given us a completely new perspective on Christ and on people.

Before the words 'the old has gone', there comes a Greek word that the NIV often does not translate, a word rendered 'behold' in a number of other versions. This is a pity, for it gives dramatic vividness to the three statements (two in verse 17 and one in verse 18) that follow.

It is as if Paul is standing once more, in his imagination, on the road to Damascus. His eyes have been temporarily blinded but new light has come into his soul. The old world has gone, a new world has come. It is not really the world that has changed, of course, but Paul himself. He is a new person with a new outlook.

Who has done this? God! 'All this is from God.'

There is possibly a link in Paul's mind between what he says here and what he wrote in chapter 4, verse 6. The new creation brings light and in that light we see everything – and especially everyone – differently.

How has God done it? By reconciling us to himself through Christ, which, as the verses that follow show, means through the death of Christ on the cross.

3. His ministry and appeal (5:18b-6:2)

Paul may appear to have moved on from the issue of his motivation but in fact he has not. The fear of the Lord was one motive, the love of the crucified Christ another, but also the gift
and calling of God constituted a third.

God 'gave us the ministry of reconciliation' (v. 18). Who
has he in mind here in his use of the word 'us'? Is he writing
about Christians generally or of himself and the Corinthians as
representing the church at large? Either of these is possible, but
(in view of 5:20-6:2) it seems more likely he has himself and
his fellow evangelists in mind at this point.

This ministry is a reconciling one, for through it God and
sinful human beings are brought together. When it is defined,
however, this is in terms of a message, a message about something that now belongs to history.

How are we to understand the first part of verse 19? Is Paul
saying, 'God was in Christ and he was reconciling the world to
himself,' or is he saying rather, 'God was reconciling the world
to himself and he did it through Christ'?

Much turns on the sense of the phrase rendered 'in Christ'
here. Should we rather translate it 'through Christ', which is a
possible way of taking it?

The context suggests the latter, for there is much here about
the death of Christ which we know was instrumental in our
salvation. On the other hand, Paul's normal use of the phrase,
which for him almost invariably means 'in Christ', suggests the
former. It is not easy to choose between the two.

Our understanding of reconciliation in this passage is deeply
affected by the words, 'not counting men's sins against them'.
The whole verse makes the Divine initiative clear, but here it
also shows that it includes forgiveness. The actual grounds of
this will appear just a little later.

The message is committed to ambassadors (v. 20). We should

not give this word too modern a sense. These days every major nation has an ambassador in the capital city of every other major nation with whom it has diplomatic relations, but this was not the case in New Testament times. The Romans would recognize no other power with whom they would have peaceful coexistence.

Yet there were ambassadors, but their function was different. When a Roman army had defeated that of some other nation, the victorious general would send an appointed ambassador into the camp of the defeated foe. He would carry with him the peace terms.

This is the function of the Christian preacher. He goes with God's peace terms, and he does so as ambassador of the God of grace who offers forgiveness to his defeated foes.

Every analogy used in the New Testament has its points of comparison and also its points of difference, because the gospel cannot be exactly like anything else. The ambassador for Christ is like the Roman army's ambassador in taking out peace terms. These come from One with all authority, and yet, amazingly, there is a pleading note in the voice of the ambassador, quite alien to the normal outlook of a victor.

Why? Because in this case the Victor loves the vanquished! Both authoritativeness and winsomeness are appropriate in preaching the gospel.

What is the significance of Paul's apparent address to his readers in 5:20 and 6:1? Is he actually intending to address them or is his language based on memories of his first visit to their city? Having stood in his imagination on the Damascus Road (see the comments on 4:6 and 5:17), is he now taking his stance again in imagination in the marketplace or the synagogue at Corinth, preaching the message of Christ?

Either an address or a memory is possible, but we need to recall that Paul was concerned, in writing his first letter to them, that some of his readers might not know the Lord at all (1 Cor 15:34; 16:22). There is plenty of room for this concern in modern preaching too. It is all too easy to assume that a congregation made up of regular church-attenders consists entirely of true personal Christians.

What was the basis of the message as Paul proclaimed it, declaring it on behalf of Christ, himself the greatest Preacher? The message concerned both the kind of person Christ is and the work he has effected for us. In verse 21, he twice refers to sin and one of these references relates to his character and the other to his work.

He says of Christ that he 'had no sin' (literally, as AV, 'knew no sin'). As Murray Harris well puts it, 'He was without any acquaintance with sin that might come through his ever having a sinful attitude or doing a sinful act. Both inwardly and outwardly he was impeccable.'[3]

In this verse, he makes a most striking and deeply moving assertion about what an early Christian writer described as a 'sweet exchange'. Here is God in his amazing grace treating Christ as a sinner so that the sinner might be treated as righteous. This is what theologians describe as 'double imputation'. Our sin was reckoned his so that his righteousness might be reckoned ours! Could substitution be more clearly or more powerfully expressed than it is here?

Matthew and Mark have both preserved for us the terrible question asked by Christ on the cross, 'My God, my God, why have you forsaken me?' (Matt. 27:46; Mk. 15:34; cf. Ps. 22:1). This is surely the deepest question ever asked and it came from the lips of no ordinary human being, but was asked by the very Son of God.

It received no answer from heaven, as Christ was bearing

---

3. 'Second Corinthians', in F. Gaebelein (ed.), *Expositor's Bible Commentary*, Vol. 10, Grand Rapids, Zondervan, *ad loc*.

the punishment for our sins. Perhaps though the nearest to an answer is given here, under the inspiration of the Holy Spirit. This is why Jesus was forsaken. Here too is the wonderful outcome for us of that forsaking.

The first two verses of chapter 6 carry on the theme of preaching and exhortation. Does Paul mean that the recipients of the gospel are not to listen to the message of grace from God without making an adequate response? Probably this is what he means. The message of God's grace had been preached, and those who received it needed to have impressed on them the urgency of accepting it with faith.

Paul urges this not simply as the preacher of a message of human devising, but as somebody whom God has actually called to work with him (cf. 1 Cor. 3:9)! He finds support for the urgency of his appeal in the Old Testament, and he quotes from Isaiah 49:8.

This verse comes from a very significant passage, which centres on the great Servant of God who was called to preach the word to Israel and the Gentiles and, as a later passage in the same book shows us (Isa. 52:13-53:12), to give his life for them. Paul saw the fulfilment of this in the gospel he preached and he underlines here the implications of phrases like 'time of my favour' and 'day of salvation'.

The age of anticipation is past, the time of fulfilment has come, and with it the urgency of receiving the message *now*! None of us dare evade the challenge of that.

Some questions for personal reflection:

1. If I examine with honesty my motives for serving Christ, how closely do they conform to those that moved the heart of Paul?

2. Am I prepared to be thought not quite right in the head if necessary because of my commitment to the gospel of Christ?

3. Do I really look at other people through the eyes of the crucified Christ?

4. Urgency and winsomeness – do they meet in my advocacy of the gospel?

9: THE QUALITIES
OF TRUE MINISTRY (6:3-10)

Every great writer or speaker is able to adapt his style to his subject matter and to his purpose in writing or speaking. In fact in some ways this is common to all of us. Read a man's letter to his wife, his application for a job, his report as secretary of the local football club and his speech at his daughter's wedding and you might think they were all by different people.

In this section of his letter Paul's form of expression has changed considerably. The verses that lead up to it have one major topic, with the apostle's language movingly expounding the great theme of reconciliation in Christ. Now his style alters radically, becoming staccato. The words do not flow in a stream, they are punched out. This does not make them any less moving, as we shall see.

1. The concern of a true servant of God (6:3,4a)
It is possible for a preacher to say 'Come to Christ!' but for his life to say 'Do not come!' Paul has shown concern earlier in the letter to make certain that his conduct would not be misunderstood by his Corinthian readers (1:12-18; 4:1,2). This concern returns now, and he makes reference to various factors which underline the authenticity of his ministry.

Such self-vindication was not palatable to him, as we shall see later, but the circumstances apparently called for it. If the credibility of the message and of the messenger are in any way related (see the comment on 5:12), there are times when this kind of exercise needs to be done, for it is essential for the message to be given a receptive hearing.

He describes himself and his fellow-evangelists as 'servants of God'. There are a number of men of God who are so described in the Old Testament, but it is more than likely that Paul

110

chose this term because his model was the great Servant of the Lord, described in Isaiah 42, 49, 50, 52-53. Who was this Servant? Our Lord (and the New Testament writers following him) saw this figure to be fulfilled in Christ himself (Matt. 8:17; 12:17-21; Luke 22:37; John 12:37-41, etc.).

In another passage, 2 Timothy 2:24-26, he also seems to be using Christ the Servant of the Lord as his model, for the picture of the kind and gentle instructor given there is so much like the One portrayed in Isaiah 42, especially in verses 2 and 3.

How does a servant of God commend himself? Not, as Paul well recognizes, simply by words, for anybody can make claims, but in at least four ways, each of which we will explore in turn.

2. The circumstances to be faced by a true servant of God (6:4b-5)

The list Paul gives here is well headed by the words, 'in great endurance'. Most of us live in a comfortable world and in circumstances of comparative ease. To be a servant of God, however, must mean readiness to suffer, for this has been the lot of so many and most of all of Christ, God's supreme Servant.

No better commentary could be made on these words than what Paul himself says in chapter 11, verses 23 to 29, where he spells out what is simply hinted at in our present passage. There can be no doubting the fact that service for Christ had been most costly for him, and it was not over yet. There would still be hardships to endure, as we see in the last eight chapters of the Acts of the Apostles, and these would include arrest by the Romans and the hair-raising journey to Rome itself. Eventually his life would end in martyrdom.

He begins with three general terms, 'troubles', a word which is wide enough to include every difficult experience, 'hardships' and 'distresses', which relate to external and internal pressures respectively.

Then come 'beatings, imprisonments and riots' which are much more specific and which can certainly be documented from what Luke tells us about Paul's life and ministry in the period up to the writing of this epistle (Acts 14:19; 16:19-24; 19:19-34). The good news of Christ had a harsh reception in many a place when it was first proclaimed. This came sometimes from the authorities, who could order beatings and prison and sometimes from unruly crowds who could make life difficult both for the evangelists and, as a result, also for the authorities.

Then come three more phrases which describe oft-recurring conditions, not in any way imposed by others, but rather self-imposed in the sense that Paul and his fellow-evangelists refused to be turned back by the privations the work involved. Hard work by day, lack of sleep at night, and periods of hunger sound more like the reminiscences of an explorer, moving through uncharted territory, having to clear a way for himself, beset with mosquitoes through the night watches and without adequate provisions for the journey. They show that being a missionary of the cross was anything but a soft option.

3. The character of a true servant of God (v. 6)

What Paul faced during his missionary travels required great character qualities. It is however worth remembering that hard experiences may also make a lasting impression on our characters, so that God may use the very afflictions we encounter to fit us to meet further trials.

Of course, there has first to be a willingness to learn through such experiences or to be moulded by God through them. 'The same heat that hardens the egg also softens the butter.' It is our attitude that makes the difference.

What were the qualities Paul sought to exemplify?

'Purity' is rightly put first, for it suggests both holiness of life and a total commitment to the Lord's work unmixed with any allegiance that would pull the other way (cf. 6:14-7:1). This is basic and non-negotiable.

'Understanding' for a Christian worker needs to be twofold, for he must understand God's truth if he is to communicate it clearly and faithfully, and he needs too to understand the people with whom God brings him into contact. Probably Paul has the second chiefly in view here, because the two items that follow it in his list are like it in being somewhat gentle qualities.

Now comes patience. Some character qualities may reveal themselves in a brief moment of time. It only takes a second or two to decide to tell the truth when a lie would be more convenient, or to act in love to save somebody from serious accident at the risk of your own life. But patience, along with some other qualities such as faithfulness, needs time to reveal itself and is all the more impressive because of this.

Kindness may seem a somewhat pale word in such a list, but this is not a correct impression. It suggests in fact an outgoing compassion that finds it natural to consider the interests of the other person and to act accordingly.

Does 'the Holy Spirit' seem an intruder in this list? If so, then perhaps we have not understood what the Christian life really is. Without his work within us there would be no Christian life at all.

The fact is that none of the character qualities of the Christian is self-produced. Every one of them is due to the work of the Spirit, the Holy Spirit, in the Christian's heart. Paul's list of the fruit of the Spirit, which he gives in Galatians 5:22,23, and which includes some of the qualities found in this passage, makes this abundantly clear. It is therefore quite apt that the Holy Spirit should have a central place in Paul's list of qualities.

What does the Holy Spirit produce? The first and greatest of his graces is love (Gal. 2:22; 1 Cor. 13:13). It may seem strange that Paul finds it necessary to say 'sincere love,' for it is often said that love cannot be counterfeited. There can be no doubt though that Satan tries to counterfeit even this. Can anything be more nauseating than a false profession of love, such as the kiss of Judas?

As we have already seen (5:14), it was love for Christ and for others, produced by Christ's love for him, that was the motive power constraining Paul during his missionary career.

4. The resources of the true servant of God (v. 7)

What does the servant of Christ have available for his work for the Lord? It is interesting to see that Paul has nothing to say here about communication techniques or physical resources. This does not mean there is no place for them, but rather that they belong very much in the second division and not in the first. In fact, the Christian's resources are intimately related to the character qualities which we have just been considering. In serving Christ, what do we give? Primarily we give the message and we give ourselves. Everything else is secondary.

Christian work is concerned primarily with the communication of a message, and this has one indispensable quality – it is true. So, whether he is in the pulpit or the marketplace, whether he is standing on trial before magistrates or chatting casually over the garden wall, the lips of the servant of God must utter only truth. To speak the truth should be completely habitual to him.

In this way the lips of Paul and his fellow-workers, because they were dedicated to Christ, became vehicles of the power of God, for, as Paul himself declared (Rom. 1:16), the gospel is itself God's power for salvation for those who believe.

Human words, no matter how true and good, are without impact apart from the power of the Holy Spirit. Paul also shows his recognition of this principle in writing 1 Thessalonians 1:4-6.

It is important to notice that when he uses an analogy in connection with the work of spreading the gospel it is often drawn from the battlefield. See Romans 6:13, Ephesians 6:11-17; 1 Thessalonians 5:8. This reveals the standpoint from which he viewed his service. Gospel communication is actually an attack on the enemy's territory and the Christian needs spiritual weapons for this.

What are these weapons? Paul does not actually say, choosing to characterize rather than identify them. They are, he says, weapons of righteousness.

What does this mean? Possibly that these weapons are given to us because of our new righteousness in Christ, through whom God has declared us righteous in his sight. On the other hand, the phrase may signify that godly character is itself a powerful weapon against the enemy, which it undoubtedly is.

We may move a little closer to identifying these weapons when we notice that they are said to be 'in the right hand and the left'. The man or woman of God needs to be able to attack and repulse Satan on all sides.

Perhaps then these weapons are really simply different aspects of God's truth contained in his Word, and so are to be regarded as equivalent to 'the sword of the Spirit, the word of God' (Eph. 6:17). To support this we might note that the verse begins with 'truthful speech'. Paul's use of the plural, 'weapons,' may mean that he is thinking of the varied material there is in Scripture, to be used for different purposes in the fight against Satan.

This is certainly what we find in the accounts of our Lord's encounter with Satan recorded in Matthew 4:1-11 and Luke 4:1-13. Even though all the quotations Jesus uses are from one section of the Old Testament, Deuteronomy chapters 6 to 8, they proved to be relevant to different temptations used by Satan against him.

5. The reaction of others to the true servant of God (vv. 8-9a)
This fascinating little section is not easy to interpret in detail
and yet its general thrust is unmistakable. Paul may be saying
that people have reacted to him in two different ways, some
honouring him and thinking well of him while others thought
him nothing better than an imposter. This is the view of some
commentators.

Others however consider that he is thinking of the world's
assessment on the one hand and that made by God on the other.
God honours his servants, thinks well of them, sees them to be
genuine, and in fact knows all about them. The world though
may often dishonour them, treat them as charlatans, give a bad
report of them, and at times may well ask 'Who are these people and who do they think they are?'

It is not easy to decide between these two interpretations, as
both make sense. It is worth remembering though that they meet
in the fact that, if human beings do honour him and see him to
be genuine, then this coincides with God's own estimate of him.

In the end it is God's assessment alone that matters, but we
need to face the fact that the world often does not view us in the
way he does. It is antagonistic towards us – or is it?

There can be no doubt that today the world does not always
view the church in the way suggested here. Far from arousing
antagonism, so often the world simply regards the church as
not worth bothering with. If we are treated as totally irrelevant,
are we really acting as salt and light as Christ intended we should
(Matt. 5:13,14)?

6. The paradoxical life of the true servant of God (9b, 10)
There is something paradoxical about the life and work of the
Christian in the world as it is. Each side of the paradox is well
worth considering in each of the pairs Paul brings before us
here.

'Dying and yet we live on' sums up Paul's own teaching in Romans 6, and he touches this also in chapter 1 of this epistle. As we are prepared to die, so a spiritual resurrection takes place. The Christian life is always life on this side of Calvary and the empty tomb, and it is only truly authentic when both feature as characteristics of it.

'Beaten and yet not killed' was true for him. Suffering there may well be, but he is still alive to carry through the commission God has given him to fulfil.

'Sorrowful yet always rejoicing' – how true! So many of the psalms in our Psalter can be classified either as laments or as hymns of praise. For the Christian the two are actually combined. Sorrow there must be, for we live in a sinful and painful world. We sorrow at the sins and pains of others, and also of ourselves. Yet there is a song in our hearts because of all Christ has done for us, and because we know that eventually, in God's good time, all the sorrows will disappear (Rev. 21:4).

'Poor yet making many rich' – Paul will show us later on that this is true, not just of the Christian, but supremely of Christ himself (8:9). He was rich yet for our sake became poor so that through his poverty we might be rich. In this way, we see that Christ epitomizes in himself every great principle of the godly life.

'Having nothing, and yet possessing everything' – this recalls a pregnant statement from Paul's First Epistle, where he says 'All things are yours' (1 Cor. 3:21). Christianity is in some ways a world-denying faith, and yet it contains great affirmatives. Because we have Christ we have all, and we rejoice together in this.

Some questions for personal reflection:

1. Do I pray for Christians who experience, as Paul did, severe persecution for Christ's sake?

2. Do I seek to understand the people among whom God has set me as a witness for him?

3. If I am to use God's word in the fight against Satan, is it enough to have it in my mind or should it be in my heart too?

4. Does my church count for Christ in its neighbourhood or do the people simply ignore it?

10: THE WINSOMENESS
AND STRICTNESS OF LOVE (6:11-7:4)

This passage contains a feature which does occur quite a lot in this letter (especially in chapters 1 and 2), but which it is easy to overlook or to ignore as of little significance. This is Paul's tendency to move from 'we' to 'I' and back again. It is a reminder to us that Paul associates Timothy with him in his opening greetings (1:1).

There can be no doubt that the doctrinal teaching of which there is so much in the letter was Paul's own, but there are many personal touches and Timothy will certainly have identified very much with Paul in these. There are also however places where Paul reverts to the singular and these are often particularly self-revealing.

In this passage, Paul and his friend show how deep is their concern for the Corinthian Christians. People in the caring professions are often warned against too much emotional involvement, and it is easy to see why this is. A pastor can however no more avoid identifying with his people in their sorrows (and, of course, their joys) than a parent can. In fact, as we shall see, Paul here describes himself as a kind of father to them. What matters, of course, both in the family and in the church, is that there should be no favouritism but that the pure love of Christ should be channelled equally to all.

We tend to go to Paul's letters very largely to learn doctrine, the wonderful truths he was commissioned to communicate. We should not forget though that there is also much we can learn from the attitudes of this Christ-centred man. He was not perfect – only the Lord Jesus was that – but his attitudes can often challenge us.

1. His desire for their responsive love (6:11-13)

Paul does not often refer to his readers by name after he has done so in his opening greeting. When he does, we can see that this reflects his feelings for them (Gal. 3:1; Phil. 4:15). He hardly needs to tell them how wide open his heart and that of Timothy are towards them, for the word 'Corinthians' shows us this (v. 11).

In so much that he has said up to this point he has spoken very freely. Whether in writing of his sufferings (1:3-11) or explaining why he has not yet re-visited them (1:12-2:5), or in showing his attitude to the man who has caused trouble (2:6-11), or in revealing what makes him 'tick' in his ministry (2:12-6:10), he has been remarkably frank. He has simply opened his heart and shown them what his feelings are. In modern parlance, he has worn his heart on his sleeve and in so doing has shown how deep is the love that is in that heart.

Much that he has written must have deeply moved the Corinthian Christians as they heard Paul's letter read out at one of their gatherings. It would be good to think that it may have won the hearts of those who were inhibited in their affection because they had been holding something against him.

In verse 13, Paul employs the kind of playful logic that might be used in a family situation, and he does this because he is like a father to them (cf. 1 Cor. 4:14-16; 1 Thess. 2:11-12). There is no doubt that to lead others to Christ can set up a special kind of bonding, for the love a parent has for a child he or she has begotten or borne has its counterpart in such a situation. He says, in effect, 'It's only right for you to open your hearts to me when I have opened mine to you.'

2. His concern for their uncompromised holiness (6:14-7:1)

At this point there is such a change of tone that many scholars have felt that what follows cannot be part of the same letter, but an insertion of some other material. It is not usually suggested that Paul did not write these words, but that he did not do so as part of this letter. This theory is fully discussed in the Introduction,[1] where it is argued that such a conclusion is not necessary. We will therefore treat this passage as part of the same epistle as what goes before and what follows it.

The change of tone is certainly very noticeable, but it is altogether consistent with Paul's assertion of his deep affection for the Corinthians. After all, real love, as distinct from its sentimentalized counterfeit, is always deeply concerned for the highest good of its beloved, and that good for God's people is holiness, likeness to Christ (Rom. 8:28, 29).

First of all he gives a very general exhortation (v. 14a), which incorporates a graphic illustration based on Deuteronomy 22:10. The Law of Moses was much more compassionate than many tend to think. At that point it forbade the yoking together of an ox and an ass for ploughing. This unequal pairing would have been painful and perhaps injurious to the animals and moreover would have produced very poor furrowing.

The illustration can hardly be applied to contacts that do not involve significant co-operation, and Paul has already made it clear in his first letter that he would not advocate a kind of monastic retreat from the world for Christians (1 Cor. 5:9, 10; 10:27). There must be some middle way between complete withdrawal from our human environment and total involvement in it, and it is surely the kind of relationship which inevitably leads to compromise that Paul has in mind.

The most obvious application, of course, is to marriage. Paul had already given practical guidance on this to the Corinthians (1 Cor. 7), making it clear that any marriage after conversion should only be with a fellow-believer (1 Cor. 7:39). The exhortation here is so general, however, that it will cover other close

---

1. See Introduction, pp. 18-21.

associations likely to involve compromise, and is therefore something every Christian must think about.

Paul now gives a series of five rhetorical questions. What most English translations fail to bring out is that the verbs used are different each time. This may be mere stylistic variation, for they are virtual synonyms. On the other hand, it could be a way Paul has of emphasizing his point by adding verb to verb in this way, the method of emphasis by accumulation. The Bible writers use many different methods of underlining the points they make.

The first two pairs are in fact very close synonyms, for light and darkness are used to symbolize righteousness and wickedness, as we see from a passage like 1 John 1:5-9, although sometimes darkness has the extra connotation of secret sin (Eph. 5:8-13).

Next come Christ and Belial, and this shows us that it is not only character qualities but personal allegiance that is in view.

In the Old Testament, the expression, 'children of Belial' occurs a number of times, as the AV brings out in passages like Deuteronomy 13:13; 1 Samuel 1:16; 2:12 and 1 Kings 21:10. There it is obviously pejorative, although its exact meaning is uncertain. The most popular view is that 'Belial' means 'worthlessness'.

After the completion of the Old Testament it came to be used by the Jews as a name for Satan. It is obviously in this sense that Paul is employing it here.

The term would, of course, still have associations with its older use. If it had meant 'worthlessness', it is not surprising that Paul now goes on to refer to a believer and an unbeliever. 'Wickedness', 'darkness' and 'worthlessness' might all seem to his readers to be inapplicable to an unbeliever of good character, so that it was most important for Paul to go this step further. It was vital that his readers should not miss the decisive character of his teaching here. An unbeliever, no matter how attractive in character, is nevertheless on the wrong side of the fence as far as God is concerned.

In his first letter to the Corinthians, Paul had made it clear that he regarded any compromise with idolatry as quite unacceptable, indeed unthinkable, for a Christian (1 Cor. 10:14-22). It was, in fact, idolatry that had been the downfall of both Israel and Judah in Old Testament times and so the freedom of the people from idolatry on their return from Babylon was undoubtedly a positive gain. How inconceivable it would have been then if Christianity had been prepared to sanction or turn a blind eye to what Judaism so rightly abhorred!

Now (v. 16b) Paul's thought takes an interesting turn, and one for which there had been some preparation in his first epistle to them. In 1 Corinthians 3:10-17 he describes the church of Christ first as a building and then more specifically as a temple (cf. Eph. 2:20-22), while later, in 1 Corinthians 6:19, he uses the term 'temple' of the body of the individual Christian.

Here he follows up this important thought by giving a catena (a connected selection of passages) from the Old Testament to give extra support to his exhortation.

The first is a great Divine affirmation (v. 16), expressing the essence of God's special covenant relationship with his people Israel. It looks as if it is a quotation from Leviticus 26:11,12, although various parts of it appear in quite a number of passages, including Exodus 6:7; 25:8; 29:45; 1 Kings 6:13; Jeremiah 32:38 and Ezekiel 37:27.

Some of these passages, especially those in Leviticus and Ezekiel, have a strong holiness context, for Israel's God was himself holy and called his people too to be holy. It is therefore not surprising that Paul's next quotation (v. 17), from Isaiah 52:11 (with a short addition from Ezekiel 20:41), is an exhortation to be separate. In its context this is a call to leave Babylon, and it is important to remember that this was not simply an oppressor but an idolatrous nation.

Now comes a wonderful promise (v. 18), which seems to be from 2 Samuel 7:14 interpreted in the light of the verse that precedes it there.

In this passage, God promises David that he will build him a house (i.e. a household or family or dynasty) and then he adds the promise that he will be a father to David's kingly son. The Epistle to the Hebrews sees 2 Samuel 7:14 to be fulfilled in Christ (Heb. 1:5), who was himself of the line of David, and Paul probably saw the promise of a house to David as fulfilled in the church, which, through Christ, becomes God's family (Gal. 3:26-28).

There may be a suggestion in this that there is no need for Christians to seek close alliances with the ungodly, for they have God as their Father and he has given them through Christ a host of brothers and sisters.

To be members of the people of God and even of the family of God – here are two wonders of grace to inspire our praise and to lead us to holiness through gratitude! So we are not surprised when the first verse of chapter 7 sums up what Paul has been saying and presses home its challenge.

Something of special significance in this verse is often overlooked. Paul says that we have these promises. This is thought-provoking, for all these promises he quotes here were originally made to Israel, not to the Christian church. So Paul appears to be assuming that the church inherits promises made to Israel.

Does this mean then that the church replaces Israel in God's plan, or does it imply rather an integration of the two, at least when Israel as a nation comes to Christ? Opinions differ, but the latter certainly seems to be suggested by the apostle's olive tree illustration in Romans 11:17-24. Whatever differences there are between Israel and the church, there is continuity between them at one level at least, because of the presence of Hebrew Christians within the church.

Paul was a big Christian thinker and, although often concerned with detail, he never lost sight of the bigger picture. We are not surprised then to find that, after dealing with the specific issue of ungodly liaisons, he makes an even broader appeal to his readers. He calls them, somewhat as he was to do a few months later with the Romans (Rom. 12:1,2), to general purification, to wholehearted holiness. The phrase, 'body and spirit', suggests outward conduct on the one hand and inner thought and attitude on the other.

The word translated 'reverence' is literally 'fear' (see the comment on 5:11), and it is perfectly apt in this context, for, although the Christian no longer has fear of condemnation, he reverences God as his Father and this motivates him in doing his holy will.

3. His joy at their godly sorrow (7:2-4)

Dividing up a Bible book into its natural sections is rarely easy, for it is rather like dissecting a plant, which is adapted, with all its parts, for growing in a field rather than lying in pieces on the botanist's table.

It is evident, however, that Paul's 'Great Digression',[2] which commenced at 2:14, comes to its conclusion at the end of 7:4, for in the next verse he returns to the subject of the return of Titus to him from Macedonia. We therefore treat verses 2 to 4 as linked to 6:11-7:1.

When we do this, we find, contrary to the views of some scholars[3], that the whole passage can be read quite naturally. Paul has declared his love for the Corinthians, he has demon-

2. See Introduction, p. 22.
3. See Introduction, pp. 18-21.

strated it in his passionate concern for their holiness, and now
he makes a further plea for an answering love on their part.

The opening plea of verse 2 simply puts the thought of 6:13
into different words. Paul's heart is open to them, now let them
open their hearts to him.

He goes on to assert that there can be no reason for them to
withhold their love from him. The three statements of this verse,
with their three verbs, 'wronged', 'corrupted', 'exploited' probably take up words that some at Corinth have used at some time,
quite unjustly, about Paul. Paul's conscience however is clear.
The charges are groundless.

In verse 3, he says, 'I do not say this to condemn you.' Paul
consistently shows amazing tact in his letters, as a reading, for
example, of his letter to Philemon shows very clearly. Here he
is concerned lest they might get the impression that he is himself levelling charges against them. The accusations against him
must have come from a small group and never shared by the
majority, although they might have made some others rather
inhibited in their dealings with him just in case they proved to
be true.

'I have said before' probably relates to 6:11. If it does, then
this provides an argument for the unity of the epistle at this
point. If, as some hold[4], 6:14-7:1 represents an intrusion from
another letter, it would seem strange for Paul to use an expression like this to point his readers to something he had said only
four verses earlier, whereas it is much more feasible if the in-
terval is as much as ten verses.

Relations with the Corinthians had been going through some
difficulties of late, but this had not in any way altered Paul's
love for them, which he believed to be deep enough to enable
him not only to share life with them but also, if need be, to face
death with them, perhaps in a situation of persecution.

---

4. See Introduction, pp. 18-21.

Verse 4 is one of the strongest positive statements Paul makes about the Corinthian Christians in his extant correspondence with them. It looks forward to what he will say soon about Titus and the news this friend of his brought back from Corinth. He had been facing troubles (see 'conflicts' in v. 5), but the news had made his heart leap for joy.

'So,' Paul must have thought, 'my work there has not been in vain after all!'

Some questions for personal reflection:

1. To what extent is it right or helpful for me to reveal my feelings to others if God has given me a ministry to them?

2. Am I involved in any relationship that compromises my commitment to Christ? If so, what should I do about it? More than that, what *will* I do about it?

3. How much do I value my place in the family of God as such and also those members of it who are joined to me in my local church?

4. Can I still love Christians I have helped even if they show no gratitude towards me?

11: PAUL'S FRIEND RETURNS TO HIM (7:5-16)

There are times when we find waiting for news almost unbearable. An examination has been taken and much depends on its result. A woman has gone into labour and her husband, unable perhaps to be with her, is eager for news of the birth. A hostage has been released and the family, long parted from him, yearns to know that it is indeed their loved one who has been freed.

Paul comes across to us in his letters as a man with common human emotions. He too found waiting difficult, in fact almost unbearable at times, and he says so quite openly and frankly.

What is so noticeable is that what he was most eager for was news of the churches. He was very much a churchman. He did not devalue the church or think only in terms of nurturing the spiritual life of individuals, important as that was. He had been used by God to establish local churches and he had them very close to his heart. There were times when he ached for news of them.

He now tells us of such a time, and in so doing he comes back to the point at which he went off at a tangent at the start of the 'Great Digression' (see the comment on 2:14). As we noted there, moving off his main theme is a characteristic of Paul's style, but we also saw that he always comes back eventually and continues along the main track.

1. He had brought comforting news (7:5-7)
Read again chapter 2, verses 12 and 13. Paul had been preaching the gospel in Troas during his third missionary journey, but he was also eagerly awaiting the arrival of Titus from Corinth and could not rest because the coming of his friend was somewhat delayed. Even after going over into Macedonia (v. 5, mentioned also by Luke in Acts 20:1), the situation had not improved. The table on page 25 seeks to set this in the context of

Paul's contacts with the Corinthian church.

In 2:13 he had written that he had no peace of mind, while here (v. 5) he says he had no rest of body. This change of language can hardly imply a contrast. Experience teaches us that mental concern can often show itself in physical restlessness. He could of course mean more than this, perhaps intending his readers to understand that he had been moving around some of the Macedonian churches looking for Titus in case his friend had paused at one of them on his return journey.

In life, pressures may come either from outside, from circumstances, from our contact with others, or from within, from our own fears and anxieties. Paul was not immune to either, and he had evidently had an unpleasant time in Macedonia. He does not say what the conflicts were. Perhaps they were due to opposition to his evangelistic preaching. The fears were probably focused on the delay in the return of Titus to him.

Paul never lost an opportunity to draw attention to the character of God, which is of course always the source of stability for godly living. Already (1:3) he has described him as 'the God of all comfort'.

The word translated 'downcast' (v. 6) means any kind of lowliness, whether of status or of emotion or of attitude, and so it is used of Christ's attitude and translated 'meekness' in 10:1. The translators have assumed that at the present point Paul is referring to emotional depression. The context suggests they are right. Some teaching on styles of spirituality seems to be based on the assumption that no Christian should ever be downcast in spirit, but this was not true to Paul's experience.

He does not tell us where he was when Titus returned to him, although we assume he was still in Macedonia. His coming was a great source of comfort to Paul. Perhaps he had been anxious about his actual physical safety. What we can be sure of is that he would eagerly enquire from him what the situation

was like in Corinth. How did they receive him, knowing of course
that he had come at the request of Paul? What was the spiritual
state of the church?

The report Titus brought to Paul was good. He had evidently
been warmly received by the Corinthian believers (v. 7) and he
had found the general situation at the church much improved.

Paul uses three phrases to describe the nature of the good
news Titus had brought.

First, there was 'your longing for me'. He has already been
seeking to rebuff the charge that he had promised to come and
yet had not fulfilled that promise. It was apparently clear though
to Titus that their concern to see Paul was very genuine. They
may have complained about his earlier non-appearance (cf. 1:15-
17), but for most of them this was because they genuinely de-
sired fellowship with him.

The reference to 'your deep sorrow' points to the genuineness of the church's repentance for any disloyalty it had shown
to him. They had not made excuses but had simply said how
very sorry they were to have caused him such pain.

The adjective used in the phrase, 'your ardent concern for
me' suggests intensiveness, zeal, passion, and perhaps means
that they were now deeply troubled at the pain they had apparently caused him.

All this was evidence of a better state of things at Corinth
and gave Paul a great increase of joy.

2. He had witnessed godly sorrow (7:8-13a)

These verses make it clear what Paul means by 'your deep sorrow' in verse 7, for it is apparent that Titus had spelled out for
him just what the outlook of the Corinthian Christians now was.

Paul's previous letter to them (v. 8),[1] had upset its recipients.
It is most interesting to see the inner conflict, the oscillation of

---

1. See Introduction.

emotions, that this caused for Paul himself.

When he first heard of their reaction, apparently, he regretted having written to them in this vein. This again shows how very human he was. None of us likes the thought that we have caused sorrow to people we love.

Yet, of course, sorrow caused by discipline may lead to action, and therefore may be for the spiritual benefit of the people concerned, and this happened in the case of the Corinthians. They did not simply lick their wounds but began to put things right. So Paul's regret was soon dispelled (vv. 8, 9). His letter to them had been used by God to accomplish what Paul himself had ardently hoped for, the putting right of the unhappy situation at Corinth.

Paul writes about 'repentance' and then goes on to give a most helpful definition of it, in so doing distinguishing it from mere remorse. All who are concerned to see Christ have his way in others, whether in evangelistic or in pastoral situations, would do well to study very carefully what the apostle says here.

The Greek word *metanoia*, 'repentance' (v. 9) means literally 'a change of mind', and it is used in the New Testament of that radical change of outlook, especially about our personal sin, that comes in the course of a saving encounter with Christ.

Paul could see that his letter to them had in fact been a means of accomplishing God's purpose. There is a proper place for sorrow in the Christian life and if we have been wayward and know we have then clearly we should feel sorry. Incidentally, this shows that genuine repentance is not simply intellectual or even volitional (although the latter is its central feature) but affects the whole personality, including the emotions.

Verse 10 is particularly illuminating. Godly sorrow has altogether a positive function, leading to all the blessings of salvation, so that when the person concerned looks back on it, it is not with resentment but rather with thanksgiving.

When Paul says that it 'leads to salvation' he is not implying that the Corinthians had lost their salvation during the time when he and they were at variance with each other. He is making a very general statement about repentance, and, of course, for those who have never been in fellowship with Christ, it introduces them to salvation, while for those who are already in Christ it restores the joy of salvation.

Worldly sorrow, on the other hand, brings death. It does so, of course, because of the deep bitterness of soul it so often brings with it, and if this persists and there is no true repentance, judgment must follow.

Paul then encourages them to reflect on their own experience of this godly sorrow that had recently come into their lives.

There follows (v. 11) a fascinating series of phrases, each composed of only two words in the Greek, the first in each case being *alla*, here well translated 'what'. The apostle who could write long flowing sentences, full of subordinate clauses, could also (as we have seen already in 6:4-10), communicate his thought in staccato form, each style being well fitted to its subject matter. Some of these phrases can only be expressed, as here in the NIV, by rather longer phrases in English.

Their 'earnestness' revealed how seriously they had taken Paul's comments on the unsatisfactory situation at the church.

Paul's reference to their 'eagerness to clear themselves', to put things right, shows how different their attitude now was from their apparent reluctance to do so at an earlier time. This then was clear evidence of their true repentance.

The 'indignation' to which he refers will have been directed towards the person in their church who was the chief cause of the problems there.[2] This was perfectly proper, for anger and love can co-exist, as every parent knows.

Their 'alarm' was, of course, because of the sorrow they

---

2. See Introduction, pp. 15, 16 and comment on 2:5-11.

now realized they had caused Paul and it was accompanied by a 'longing' to see him face to face. It is often only in such personal encounter that we are fully satisfied that reconciliation has been fully effected between ourselves and another party.

The concluding phrase, 'readiness to see justice done,' perhaps testifies to Paul's warm approval of the fact that their repentance had proved to be much more than an emotional reaction. They had been prompted to take action that would put the matter right.

The concluding sentence of this verse can hardly mean, as some commentators have thought, that the Corinthians had managed to persuade Titus that they had been without guilt. This certainly fits very ill with what Paul has said about their deep sorrow and about their repentance. He must mean that they had proved themselves now to be innocent by clearing the matter up once and for all.

As Paul has already said (vv. 6-9), what Titus reported of attitudes and events at Corinth had greatly comforted him, and, he now says, encouraged him. Probably he means that he can now see that his ministry among them, both in person and through letters, has not been in vain but that God has truly been at work in it. This must have warmed his heart considerably.

3. He had enjoyed refreshing fellowship (7:13b-16)

I once saw a Christian man who showed, by his body language, the deep dejection of his spirit. He had just been visited by the representative of a missionary society. This man had been charged with the sad task of telling him that his application to the society had been turned down. Incidentally, he is now, years later, very happily engaged in work with that same society. At that time, though, every line of his body showed the deep disappointment he was experiencing.

Perhaps Paul noticed the body language of Titus when they

met after Paul's search for him, so that he may have seen (for it is a verb of sight he uses here in v. 13b) the joy in the bearing of his friend even before he told him what had transpired at Corinth.

Translations of the Bible into English are sometimes subject to slight revisions, and this is true of the NIV here. Earlier editions of it read, '.... how happy Titus was, because all of you helped put his mind at ease', while later read '.... how happy Titus was, because his spirit has been refreshed by you all.'

This is probably an improved translation, for in verse 14 Paul seems to be moving beyond the particular problem that had been concerning him, and to be referring to the way he had commended the Corinthian believers so broadly to Titus before the latter had started out on his mission to that church. His actual experience there had given refreshment or rest to his spirit. In other words, he had greatly enjoyed their fellowship and had left them rested in spirit.

Paul had been concerned that the Corinthians should not think him untruthful and therefore unreliable (1:12-2:1). He had also apparently felt some embarrassment lest, when Titus had arrived at Corinth, he had found the Corinthians less warm and brotherly and responsive than Paul had said they were.

This apprehension about possible embarrassment had proved unfounded. So, both as regards what he had said to the Corinthians and also what he had said to Titus, Paul's words had proved to be true. His relief at this was quite proper, for a Christian who may not normally be too troubled about false reports concerning him, is right to be concerned if he gets a reputation, even a false one, for untruthfulness, particularly if he is a preacher of the true Word of the true and living God.

What a strange situation! Titus must have gone to Corinth with a real fear in his mind that he, an emissary of Paul, would not be well received by the believers in that city. Yet, at the very same time, those Christians were also fearful, for they wondered whether they could satisfy him that all was well! Such a situation can still occur in church circles today.

What is the obedience to which Paul refers here? Probably (and this may be true also of the similar verse in Philippians 2:14), he is referring to some communication that came from him to them by way of Titus, some word from the Lord. Perhaps it was an application of Old Testament Scripture to the situation. If so, he would then have challenged them to be obedient to what God was saying to them.

Evidently they had received this message very fully and acted on it in obedience. This made the heart of Titus go out to them in love. When an obedient Christian encounters the obedience of others, that person's heart is greatly warmed, knowing that he or she is among members of the loving and obedient family of God.

Verse 16 rounds off all Paul has written here. The Corinthians needed to have complete confidence in him, and he wanted, for his part, to have complete confidence in them. The visit of Titus to them, and their reception of him and response to his ministry, had completely reassured him.

Some questions for personal reflection:

1. Do I value the Church in general and my church in particular as highly as God does – or even as Paul did?

2. If I meet a Christian today who is depressed by circumstances in his own life, how can I best help him?

3. How can I make clear, in my gospel witness, the nature and importance of repentance?

4. If all I need is provided in Christ, is it unspiritual to long for fellowship with other believers?

12: GREAT EXAMPLES
OF LIBERALITY (8:1-15)

The quality of a Christian's discipleship may be measured in a number of ways. How concerned is he for the glory of God? What is the quality of her prayer-life? What kind of appetite does he have for the Word of God? Has she a concern to reach others for Christ?

There is another important test that can be applied. What about his or her attitude to money? The work of God needs finance, for Christian workers have to live, and buildings for purposes of worship, evangelism and teaching cost money, even if they are rented. Then there is the cost of Bibles and literature, of necessary fares, and many other ways in which money needs to be spent in the service of Christ.

To say then that money does not matter is not a proper Christian spirituality but a naive 'super-spirituality'. God created material things, as the very first chapter of the Bible tells us, and we need to use them for his glory and for the progress of his gospel.

More likely than this super-spirituality, however, is the materialism that can find its way into our hearts because we live in a grasping society and are not immune to the temptation to accumulate material things. In fact, if we live in a community where material possessions are highly regarded and are even used at times as the measure of a person's value ('how much is he worth?'), it is easy for that attitude to rub off on us.

It is therefore good that in an epistle where so much relates to Christian service, Paul takes two chapters to deal with this sensitive and important issue.

The background to these chapters is the collection Paul was making among the churches for the poor people among the Hebrew Christians at Jerusalem. He mentions his concern for the poor in Galatians 2:10 and refers to this particular collection in Romans 15:25-27.

There were probably several causes of this poverty. The church would experience social ostracism from the Jewish community because it worshipped a Man who was executed on a Roman gibbet, and this would certainly have economic consequences. Then there was the fact that the people of Judaea had to pay taxes both to the Jewish and to the Roman authorities.

Of course, the famine of AD 46, predicted by Agabus (Acts 11:27-30), would have been a major cause of their poverty. It is true that it had taken place about a decade ago, but we need to remember that Paul had been active for something like five years in getting this money together. In any case recent history has shown us how long it may take a community to recover from a severe famine. If, for instance, the famine had affected the crop of olives, this would have had a very serious effect on a city that looked on the Mount of Olives, crammed with olive trees just beyond its gates, as its chief economic source.

In 1 Corinthians 7-16, Paul takes up various questions the Corinthians had put to him in a letter and answers them. It is clear from chapter 16, verses 1 and 2, that they had asked for advice about the collection, and so it is obvious he had already asked them to contribute.

It is impossible to read the next two chapters of this Second Epistle without realizing that something had gone wrong and that Paul felt concerned. The larger commentaries all discuss the various possible reasons for this.

It seems most likely that Paul's critics at Corinth had expressed disapproval of his financial plans, and that they may even have misrepresented his motives. We should not however exaggerate or misunderstand the situation, for, as these chapters show, Paul assumes that the will to give was still there and simply needed to be stimulated by his letter.

1. The Macedonians and their giving (1-5)

The country we know as Greece consisted then of two Roman provinces, Achaia which had Corinth as its capital and Macedonia (extending somewhat beyond modern Greece), the capital of which was Thessalonica.

The Macedonian churches seem to have been particularly dear to Paul's heart. It is impossible to read his letters to the Philippians and to the Thessalonians without realizing this. Perhaps it was due to the fact that both churches were born out of severe persecution so that the new Christians and he were bound together by the pressure that had been imposed on them from outside.

Paul might praise a church or an individual, but he recognized that qualities of character in a Christian or a local church are not self-induced but are the product of God's grace (cf. 9:14). Here he sees this to be the case with the generosity of the Macedonian churches. The God who is supremely generous delights to impart that quality to his people.

But how are such graces created? Often in a furnace of affliction. Severe trial and extreme poverty hardly seem likely parents for such offspring as overflowing joy and rich generosity (v. 2), but if we have not recognized the element of paradox in the Christian life we have not begun to understand it. In fact, it involves an even deeper paradox, for, as Paul himself teaches earlier in this letter, for the Christian, life comes out of death (4:10,11).

He now makes three points about the generosity of the Macedonians.

First of all, he says that it was truly sacrificial. They gave 'beyond their ability' (v. 3), which can only mean they were prepared to go short of what people would regard as essentials in order to give.

In the second place, he says that they took the initiative in the matter. He had not raised the issue with them, perhaps in view of the fact that he knew they were so poor, but they had 'urgently pleaded' (v. 4) to be allowed to participate.

The expression, 'the privilege of sharing' uses two of the New Testament's loveliest nouns. The NIV translates *charis* (normally rendered 'grace') as 'privilege' here. The use of this word is most significant, for it shows, as do other passages, that Paul regarded Christian service as well as Christian salvation as a gift bestowed by God on undeserving sinners. He has much to say about this in his letter to the Ephesians (3:7-9; 4:7-13).

'Sharing' translates *koinonia*, often rendered 'fellowship'. Christian fellowship has many dimensions, but its genuineness is suspect if those who profess it close their hearts to other Christians.

In fact, thirdly and finally, the Macedonians had gone even further (v. 5). It seems as if the sense of call they felt and that impelled them to give to others had been used by God to bring them to a very deep level of commitment. This commitment was first of all to the Lord and then to Paul. This must mean that they placed themselves utterly at the Lord's disposal, and that they saw offering to help Paul in any way they could as a means of channelling their dedication to God's great purpose.

This kind of sacrificial giving is not dead in churches situated in that part of Europe. In 1992 I was teaching a group of Christians from different parts of Bulgaria, one area of which was originally within the Roman province of Macedonia. Many of the Bulgarian Christians were poor and, in economic terms, they found life hard. As they were about to go back to their own local churches at the end of the course, a senior Christian woman made a moving plea for them to urge those churches to give financially to help the suffering people of former Yugoslavia. They gladly agreed to do this.

2. The Corinthians and their giving (6, 7)

Because the Macedonians, in their poverty, had been so sacrificial, Paul had no hesitation in urging Titus to encourage the Corinthians to fulfil their promise. He may well be implying, by the way he connects their giving with that of the Macedonians, that it was much easier for them than it was for their brother Christians in that province. It seems that they were much better off.

When did Titus first broach the subject with the Corinthians on Paul's behalf? There is no means of telling, except that it must have been before Paul had sent First Corinthians to them, for he mentions it in that letter as something about which they already knew (1 Cor. 16:1, 2).

As far as they were concerned, the collection among the Corinthians would be just as much an 'act of grace,' that is, a product of God's grace in their lives, as it had been with the Macedonians (8:1).

Verse 7 gives us a fascinating Pauline perspective on the church at Corinth, many-sided but all expressed within the scope of one sentence. It bears a striking resemblance to 1 Corinthians 13. As they had already received that epistle, could it be that Paul intended by these words to remind them of the teaching he had given there?

They not only possessed but excelled in faith and knowledge (cf. 1 Cor. 13:2). They also excelled in speech (1 Cor. 13:1) and, as he has already said, their earnestness could not be questioned (7:11). They had also shown love, that virtue which was both supreme and indispensable (1 Cor. 13:13), and moreover it was love for the apostle himself. They now had a further opportunity for demonstrating love in a very practical way, not this time to him, but to their fellow-believers in Jerusalem.

3. The Lord Jesus Christ and his giving (8, 9)

If verse 7 was, in Paul's mind, consciously evocative of 1 Corinthians 13, it is not surprising that he should go on to write of Christ, in whom the love there extolled was shown to perfection. In fact it has been suggested that if Christ's name were to be substituted for the word 'love' throughout 1 Corinthians 13, it would fit perfectly.

The apostles had their place as authoritative teachers of the church and they were appointed to this work by the risen Lord himself. They cannot however furnish a model for a strongly authoritarian doctrine of Christian leadership. They certainly did not exercise an iron rule over every aspect of the church's life. They had a special place in communicating essential truth, but they did not set up any kind of ecclesiastical dictatorship.

Paul is not here commanding but rather encouraging the Corinthians to give. As an apostle, he was able to command them, as we see in 10:8 and 13:10, but he would not do so in such a matter as this, for now their motivation was all-important.

To test the sincerity of love is not necessarily to cast doubt on it. After all, Christ himself was tested in the wilderness temptations, and showed his total commitment to his Father's will. Rather, it is to give love the opportunity of showing its reality. Not everybody fears examinations, for some welcome them as presenting convincing evidence of their ability.

Paul often points his readers to Christ as the supreme Example of some virtue he is commending to them (cf. 10:1; Rom 15:1-3; Eph. 5:2; Phil. 2:1-11). The reason for this is probably partly theological, for he was convinced of the perfection of Christ in every sphere, but it was also due, of course, to the fact that he was such a Christ-centred man and so it was natural for his mind to turn to Christ no matter what subject was under discussion.

'Grace' here is used in a different although related fashion to the way Paul uses it elsewhere in this passage, for Christ is in fact the Source of grace (cf. 1:2), not simply its great Exemplar. It has greater fulness of meaning here, for he is not simply writing of a quality in Christ's character, but of the whole fact of his voluntary poverty, his entry into our human existence. As Roy Clements puts it, here the incarnation of Christ is 'not spelled out in theological detail, but encapsulated in a single metaphor'.[1]

In fact, there can be little real doubt that Paul is not here thinking simply of the conditions of Christ's earthly life, such as his birth in a manger, the few possessions he had and the fact that he was stripped even of these by the Roman execution party. There was an even deeper poverty which the incarnation made possible, that stark 'poverty' which the cross itself represented, for there he had nothing, not even fellowship with the Father he loved and who loved him. See how Paul describes the meaning of the cross in 5:21.

The word 'rich' must relate to Christ's pre-incarnate life (cf. Phil. 2:6; John 17:1, 6), for it was never true of his life on earth. This in itself suggests that becoming poor must be coextensive with Christ's whole earthly experience, from the cradle to the grave.

Through Christ the Corinthians had become rich, and this reminds us of the illustration of the treasure jars which he has given earlier in his letter (4:6, 7). Paul's use of superlatives, both in this epistle and elsewhere, and of words like 'abundance', testifies to his conviction of the great fulness of the salvation God has given us through Christ.

---

1. Roy Clements, *The Strength of Weakness*, p. 177.

4. The importance of completion (10-12)

Here too Paul is not commanding but advising (v. 10; cf. v. 8). He pays tribute to them, not only as the first to begin to give (perhaps by comparison with the Macedonians), but also as the first to express a desire to do so. There could then be no question of cajoling the unwilling but rather of facilitating the giving of the willing. All they need now do is take steps to collect the money together (v. 11).

He has said that the Macedonians gave beyond their means (v. 3). Of course, he would never put pressure on a church to do this, but would ask simply that their giving should be according to their means.

Verse 12 establishes a very important principle, already illustrated concretely by our Lord, when he said that the poor widow's two coins were worth more than the much larger offerings of the rich (Luke 21:1-4). Paul has already stated the same principle to them in his First Epistle in saying that a person's giving should be 'in accordance with his income' (1 Cor. 16:2).

5. The importance of equality (13-15)

Paul may now be anticipating an objection to the collection project. He is looking for no reversal of financial status between the Corinthians and the Jerusalem Christians (v. 13). He is concerned though that they should move somewhat closer to equality.

Verse 14 contemplates the possibility, not of the deliberate reversal of financial status but rather of a providential reversal. It was not impossible that one day the Corinthians would be in financial need and that the Jerusalem church (presumably along with others) would see that need and show their own generosity in helping to meet it.

Paul now turns to the Old Testament to find backing for his thought here. He finds it in the story of the manna, recorded in

Exodus 16:13-36. All the people gathered the manna, and they had to do it on a daily basis, but they discovered that each had according to need. As in Israel's early history, so would it be in the Christian church.

Some questions for personal reflection:

1. Paul uses the Macedonian churches as examples to the church at Corinth in the matter of generous giving. Could he have used my church in the same way?

2. It has been said that our attitude to money is a major test of our spirituality. Is this true, and, if so, what does it say about the quality of my own spiritual life?

3. Do I regard giving as a privilege or a burden?

4. Paul's mind turned to Christ so readily and so naturally no matter what the subject with which he was dealing. Is this true of me too?

13: PAUL'S FRIEND
RETURNS TO THEM (8:16-9:5)

By any standards, Paul was a great man. His gifts were so many-sided and he had that single-mindedness and enormous capacity for hard work that invariably accompany greatness in any sphere of life. He may well have made his mark in history even if he had not become a Christian.

Sometimes however a great man or woman has a certain aloofness of manner, and in contact with them we are aware that they are surrounded by an atmosphere of inaccessibility. It is true that this is sometimes accentuated by the feelings of others who, approaching a distinguished person with awe, actually set up a barrier unnecessarily. In other cases, however, the aloofness is real.

Rudyard Kipling clearly regarded this as a flaw, for, in his poem, *If*, he says, 'If you can walk with kings, nor lose the common touch, if all men count with you but none too much .... yours is the world and all that's in it, and what is more, you'll be a man, my son.'

As we read Paul's letters, and especially one like Second Corinthians which contains so much self-revelation, we see that Paul, for all his greatness, was anything but aloof. Already we have seen this feature in his moving appeal to the Corinthians to open their hearts to him because, as he said, his heart was so open to them (6:11-12).

In our present passage, we discover how warm were his feelings not only towards the members of the churches he had been instrumental in founding, but also towards the members of his team. This group of men was a brotherhood. He was its leader but it was a brotherhood nevertheless.

1. Titus and his companions (8:16-24)

Earlier in the epistle, Paul had referred to letters of recommendation and he said that he had no need of one, because the work God had done in the Corinthian church itself was like such a letter in his case (3:1-3). Here however he writes what is in effect a letter of recommendation commending three men to the church there.

The reason for this is surely that, as we shall see, the impending visit of these three to Corinth was of such an official nature and with such responsibilities that Paul seems to have felt character references to be desirable.

Yet there is one puzzling fact associated with this, for one at least of these, Titus, the Corinthians already knew well. Why then did Paul need to write about him? Perhaps the other two might have felt it strange had there been no mention of the qualifications of Titus when Paul was taking pains to spell out their own.

Paul's awareness of the significance of God's grace in the Christian life and in Christian service is most marked in this epistle. Here, for instance (v. 16), he mentions the concern Titus has for the Corinthians, but he attributes the origin of this to God.

At first it looks as if verse 17 contradicts what Paul says in 8:6. There, he says that he urged Titus to go back to Corinth and complete arrangements for the church's gift towards the collection for the Jerusalem Christians. Here it appears that the initiative in this was taken by Titus himself.

Probably what actually happened was that Paul found, on approaching Titus about the matter, that he had already been aware of an urge from God to go. So often today, two Christian people, a married couple for instance, will find that God is speaking to each of them independently about some piece of service for Christ, whether this is to be done by both or by one.

Now (8:18-24), Paul begins to refer to the two men who will travel with Titus. He does so without naming them. Discussion has turned, not only on the identity of these men, but also on the reasons for Paul's silence about their names.

Perhaps Titus was to be the leader of the group, and Paul may have felt that he would be marking him out as such by the fact that his friend would need to introduce the others to the Corinthians on their arrival at the church. An over-subtle interpretation? Probably not, for Paul's correspondence is characterized by a marked concern for courtesy.

There is little point in theorizing about their identity as we do not have adequate material to enable us to make this identification. Luke's name appears in commentaries more often than others, and it is not impossible that he was one of the two, but we will probably never be sure.

As Paul appears to have been in Macedonia when he wrote this letter,[1] it seems likely that these two brothers are themselves Macedonian Christians, especially as the Christians in that province have already figured in what Paul has said in this chapter about the collection.

The first man apparently had a ministry of some sort in more than one church (v. 18). We know of the Philippian, Thessalonian and Berean churches in Macedonia, but there may have been others in the province. Here is further evidence, from the Corinthian epistles, that there was among Christians a sense of oneness that transcended local church boundaries (see e.g. 1 Cor. 1:2; 2 Cor. 1:1). It is important for us to maintain or recapture this in our church life today.

Both Paul's comment and his reference to the churches' praise of this brother also make us aware that it is not necessarily unspiritual to recognize the value of a Christian's contribution to the Lord's service. Of course this must be balanced by Paul's comments on himself and Apollos in 1 Corinthians 3:1-9 and

---

1. See the table, 'Chronology of Paul's Contacts with the Church at Corinth' on page 25.

especially his almost contemptuous and repeated 'what...?' (not 'who...?') in verse 5 there.

Verses 18 and 19 show that we should not drive too sharp a wedge between spheres of spoken ministry and of administrative responsibility, for this brother clearly had notable involvement in both. The churches (presumably those in Macedonia) had chosen him to accompany Paul in carrying their offering to Jerusalem.

In typical fashion, Paul viewed the offering as being first of all for the glory of the Lord (the literal meaning of the phrase translated here as 'to honour the Lord'). It was also of course to provide real financial help for the Christians who would receive it.

Paul was most concerned (v. 20) that everything should be done with an eye not only to financial fidelity but also to the need for maintaining an impeccable outward testimony in relation to it. No treasurer of a church or a Christian society should have sole responsibility for finance. This is not because Christians cannot be trusted, but in order to preserve the church's reputation for integrity. Everything must be completely above board and so above suspicion even from the most cynical observer.

Paul's phrase, 'this liberal gift', may be a reference to the total offering from all the churches, or to that of the Macedonian churches. If he intends it to refer to the offering of the Corinthians, it may be intended as a tactful encouragement to them to give generously.

Paul now goes on to write about the other brother (vv. 22-24). What he says about him is of a very general although positive character. He also mentions this Christian brother's great confidence in the Corinthians. Perhaps he has already visited the church at some earlier time or has friends who have visited it. We do not know.

Now (v. 23) Paul shows that he realizes he needs to make some kind of distinction between Titus and the other two brothers who will be travelling with him. All of them are brothers in the Lord but they do not have the same function.

The apostle describes Titus as his partner and fellow-worker (cf. Rom. 16:21), and this underlines Paul's warm relationship with those who worked with him in evangelism and in the care of the churches. Titus will therefore be working at Corinth as part of that spiritual enterprise which Paul leads.

The other two brothers have a different function. The word translated 'representatives' is that normally translated as 'apostle' in the New Testament. The term means an envoy, and a distinction in the New Testament needs to be made between those who were apostles of Christ (like the Twelve and Paul) and those who were apostles of local churches, sent to represent them for a specific purpose, like the two referred to here.

This is not a subtle distinction but an important one, for the apostles of Christ had a special function in the establishment of the whole church on a gospel foundation (Eph. 2:19, 20).

The two apostles of the churches to whom Paul refers here are 'an honour to Christ', or, more literally, 'the glory of Christ'. The thought here is somewhat similar to what Paul says about Christians adorning the doctrine (AV) or 'making the teaching about God our Saviour attractive' (NIV) by their lives in Titus 2:10. It is interesting to discover that this somewhat parallel verse occurs in a letter to Titus, who appears so prominently in our present passage.

Paul was eager for these men to be well received (v. 24). Here was an opportunity for the Corinthian church to demonstrate its love for Christ in practical ways (cf. v. 8).

Paul had spoken to these men about the Corinthian church with loving pride, and he was keen that, through the visit of their representatives the Macedonian churches (for it must be these he has in mind) would see clear evidence of their love for Christ.

2. The purpose of their visit (9:1-5)
These verses are closely linked with the final verse of the last chapter, for Paul is still thinking about the kind of impression the Corinthian church will make on the Macedonian visitors when they arrive.

It might seem that he is over-concerned about this, and yet we can see that it is one of his ways of stimulating the Corinthians to generous giving and to get their gifts together soon. He is saying in effect, 'If you love me, you won't let me down.' This may not be the highest motive for giving, but it is surely a legitimate one.

Paul sometimes says that he has no need to write to a church about a particular matter and yet he goes ahead and does exactly that (cf. 1 Thess. 4:9; 5:1)! The reason, of course, is that he wants to underline something they already know or are already doing. A good teacher not only seeks to impart new truth or to encourage new endeavour, but also to underline the importance of certain truths or actions so as to establish habits of thought or life.

Just as fellowship has many forms, so also does service, and the term *dikaionia* ('service') which Paul uses here he also employs for various spiritual activities within the church, as he did, for instance, in writing 1 Corinthians 12:5. We should never imagine that giving material aid is inferior to other activities we might consider more spiritual. If it is a product of the love of Christ, there could be nothing more spiritual.

It becomes clear as we follow these verses through that Paul is not so much concerned that the Corinthians have reneged on their former pledge of help. He is still persuaded of its genuineness and of the generosity which prompted it, but he is afraid that the gift has not yet been organized.

The Corinthians had evidently shown great enthusiasm when the matter of the collection had been first raised by Paul, and this had provided a real challenge to the Macedonians. Paul himself intends to visit them, and it may be that there will be Macedonians with him. For fear of embarrassment then, let them have everything ready by the time he arrives on the scene.

Paul mentions both his possible embarrassment and theirs, and so there is in his words a double inducement to them to be prepared. He makes it clear in verse 5 that this is one of the reasons his deputation of three (9:16-24) is coming to them. They are to organize the collection.

Twice he uses the phrase 'a generous gift'. The Greek expression is very rich in meaning, and in addition to the sense given to it in the NIV can cover God's blessing of people, either directly or through others, or else an act stimulating praise to God. Perhaps Paul uses it for this reason, because all these senses would be appropriate in this context, although his second use of the phrase contrasts it with a gift grudgingly given, so that this imparts a somewhat more explicit sense to its second use here.

Some questions for personal reflection:

1. Do I regard other Christians with whom I serve the Lord as a brotherhood and how appreciative of them am I?

2. What value do I give to courtesy in my dealings with others? Is it just a comparatively unimportant and optional extra or is it a vital expression of my Christian character?

3. Is my giving to the Lord's work planned or haphazard? How can I improve my stewardship of finance?

14: THE BLESSEDNESS
OF LIBERALITY (9:6-15)

Harvest thanksgiving services seem to be somewhat out of fashion these days.

Some of us remember Sundays when the church building had a delicious smell we could often detect even before we went through the front door. The area near the pulpit was a sight for sore eyes. Masses of fruit and vegetables had been brought in during the Saturday afternoon and those who had something of an artistic flair had arranged them all to make a beautiful display. In the centre was a specially made harvest loaf. Sometimes it seemed that almost every square inch of that part of the church was crammed to capacity, and the ledges under the windows often carried the surplus.

Why is it that so many churches no longer have them? Perhaps it is because somehow tins of carrots and even bags of pre-packed apples do not look quite the same. We would certainly have some problems with frozen food and of course some of us wondered at one time if our diet might eventually turn out to be little more than vitamin pills! Imagine the church platform arranged like a chemist's shop!

I am reluctant to suggest that there could be another reason, that we have forgotten our dependence on the land and even take God's provision of our daily food very much for granted.

It is not without significance that Paul here links harvest and thanksgiving very closely to each other. It is true that he is not writing altogether literally, but there is an assumption in what he says that there are principles of seasonal sowing and harvesting, followed by thanksgiving, that apply to all life, and that the Christian needs to remember.

In verse 5, he twice uses the expression 'generous gift' in relation to the collection the Corinthians have promised to make for the poor Christians of Jerusalem. This collection is still in view right to the end of the chapter, but Paul constantly has in mind the more general spiritual principles underlying it, principles of spiritual harvest, and these are of application still today.

1. Plentiful harvest (6-10)

The words which introduce verse 6, 'Remember this' or, more literally, 'and this' introduce a double statement that has the kind of form that would suggest this is a popular proverb. Whether originating in Christian circles or from the Greek environment which formed the background to Corinthian culture, it certainly has its Biblical counterparts, especially in the Book of Proverbs (e.g. Prov. 11:24, 25) and the principle of it, minus its agricultural setting, is in the teaching of our Lord recorded in Luke 6:38. It is a fundamental law of spiritual economics. Paul uses the sowing and harvesting analogy elsewhere, with a somewhat different application, in Galatians 6:7-10.

In verse 7 he turns aside briefly to enunciate another important principle. It is not only what we give that matters but the reason for our giving.

It may have seemed to his Corinthian readers that he was seeking, in what he had already written, to put pressure on them to give. He implies here that this is not in fact the case. He has not been attempting to over-ride their wills, for voluntariness was of the essence of the matter. He has not been writing to dictate what they should do, but rather his communication is to their hearts, for it is from their hearts that decisions about giving must come.

This verse indicates too that the amount of a gift needs to be the result, not of impulse but of thoughtful decision. Good stewards of another person's property should give careful thought to matters of expenditure.

The words, 'God loves a cheerful giver,' seem to reflect Proverbs 22:8, 9, where the same analogy of sowing and reaping occurs and where the Septuagint (the leading Greek version of the Old Testament in Paul's day), has a slightly longer text than the Hebrew, including words we may translate as 'God praises (or blesses) a cheerful and generous giver'. Both in Proverbs and here in 2 Corinthians we see the importance of motivation. Paul also links generosity and cheerfulness fairly closely in Romans 12:8.

We noted earlier how often, in the first chapter of this letter, Paul indicates that God is the Source, not only of all blessing for the Christian, but of all the spiritual qualities of his life. We find the same emphasis here in verse 8. Not only does God love the cheerful giver, but he, the God of unparalleled generosity, has himself made that person's generosity possible by his grace.

In this verse, Paul underlines very strongly the total character of God's provision, for the Greek word *pas* ('all') in various forms occurs five times in this one verse, if we include the word translated 'at all times', which is a compound including *pas*. That this is deliberate emphasis is unmistakable, for in the Greek three of the five occurrences are in fact consecutive words.

He also twice uses one of his favourite words, *perisseuein* ('abound') so that the whole verse presents a picture of a God of overflowing generosity who, by that generosity, reproduces something of the same quality of character in his church.

In the context supplied by verse 6, we see that God's activity in grace here results first in provision of the needs of the Corinthian believers and then, through them, the supply of the needs of others. It assumes that inner experience of God's grace will lead to the use of excess material blessings to supply the needs of others. A challenging thought!

Now (verse 9) Paul quotes Scripture, from Psalm 112:9. 'He .... his .... his' refer, not to God, but to a particular type of man.

This Psalm is rather like an amplified version of Psalm 1, which lays down the basic principle that God blesses the righteous but judges the wicked.

If Paul intended his readers to recall the Old Testament context, this would illustrate the principle laid down in verse 8 here, for it has much to say about the material blessings God will give to those who fear him.

In the Old Testament much is made of the attitude of the rich man to the poor, as for instance in contrasting verses in Proverbs 22:9, 16, and this is in fact a major criterion distinguishing the righteous from the wicked.

This is the point being made in the verse Paul quotes. Does it seem like a statement of justification by works? If so, we should remember that Paul has already indicated that all this is the product, not of human effort, but of the grace of God (v. 8).

This point finds still more support in verse 10. Whether in literal or spiritual agriculture, both sowing and reaping can be undertaken only because of God's own generosity.

The words, 'seed to the sower and bread for food' are an almost exact quotation from the Septuagint of Isaiah 55:10, a passage Paul may well have reflected on because it applies the principles of sowing and reaping to the declaration of the word of God and its results. Here the analogy is re-applied, quite appropriately, to Christian giving. Those who give generously will be recompensed by God with resources of seed to enable them to give.

'The harvest of righteousness' surely looks back to the quotation from Psalm 112:9 given in verse 9. Just as we did there, we need to remind ourselves here that all this is based on the grace of God to which Paul refers in verse 8. God enables his people to do righteous deeds of generosity by supplying them with the means for such generosity.

2. Overflowing thanksgiving (11-15)

Paul had a firm grasp of the fact that God deals with us in grace, pouring out his blessing on us, so that we in turn may prove to be a blessing to others. In 1:4-7, he illustrates this principle in relation to comfort in affliction; here he relates it to material blessings.

The words, 'in every way' and 'on every occasion' (v. 11), demonstrate how far-reaching Paul sees this principle to be. It also shows that he is not thinking simply of the collection he is making but is establishing an important general principle of the Christian life.

At the close of this verse another important idea is introduced. The generosity of the Corinthians will, of course, be channelled through Paul and those who will travel with him to Jerusalem, and it will result in thanksgiving to God.

This demonstrates once again the apostle's God-centredness. In Romans 15:9-12, he writes about God's purpose that the Gentiles should glorify God for his mercy, and he illustrates this by quoting a number of passages from the Old Testament. He obviously longed to find men and women of every nation giving praise to God. Here he writes in similar vein about the Jerusalem Christians, who were, of course, Jews.

Evidently he anticipated that the fact others would be glorifying God would itself motivate the Corinthian Christians. Any Christian believer will be glad when God receives the praise that is due to his holy name.

This means then that their generosity will accomplish a three-fold result, for the recipients will benefit, they will themselves be blessed and the God they love and serve will be glorified.

The word Paul chooses in verse 12 to express the *performance* of their service normally has implications of voluntariness, so that Paul here seems to be reminding them of what he had said in verse 7.

The rest of the verse may seem simply to repeat and so emphasize the thought of verse 11, but in fact there are three extra touches, for totally equivalent repetition is rare in his writings.

First of all, he refers to the Jerusalem Christians as 'God's people', literally 'the saints'. This term was used of those whom God had set apart for himself in Old Testament days, but it came also to be applied to the Christian church in the New Testament. Of course, used of the Jerusalem Christians, it could bear both senses, for they were both Jews and Christian believers.

Also, this service overflows, and Paul here uses again the same favourite word he employed twice in verse 8. Like the feeding of the five thousand, itself an expression of gracious generosity, there would be more than enough for the people who were to be the immediate recipients of this act of love.

The overflow, it seems to be suggested, will affect each of the recipients, for they will all overflow with thanksgiving to God. It is not simply the Jerusalem church meeting for praise but the individual believers giving thanks in their homes that Paul may have in view here.

Verse 13 is particularly interesting, for it may come out of a realization on Paul's part that the Jerusalem Christians were probably a little concerned as to the genuineness of the faith of the Corinthian converts. After all, Corinth had a most unsavoury reputation. This had spread far beyond its city limits and may have reached Jerusalem itself. Not only so, but, as 1 Corinthians shows us, Paul had some concerns himself about certain things that were happening in the Corinthian church and the Jerusalem church may have got wind of them too.

Two qualities of the service of the Corinthians to the Jerusalem Christians were marks of the genuineness of their faith, in which they had 'proved' themselves.

The first was that it showed their obedience. True faith, as not only James but also Paul shows clearly (James 2:14-26; Rom. 6), always demonstrates itself in works and these works are of course undertaken in obedience to the will of God. The Old Testament with its many indications of God's concern for the poor and the obligation of God's people to supply their needs, may be in Paul's mind, for the Old Testament was of course the authoritative Scripture for the church as a whole. Or it may be that, in connection with the ethical teaching that was given to new converts (Acts 2:42; Rom. 6:17), there had been some reference to this.

It is not only rectitude of conduct that should characterize the Christian believer, of course, but also love. In both, he will demonstrate his new membership of God's family, for these are qualities of God himself. Generosity is itself, when properly motivated, a manifestation of love.

The Corinthians are said here to have shared with the Jerusalem saints but also 'with everyone else'. Whatever can Paul mean by this latter expression?

Perhaps he is thinking of the role of the Jerusalem church in being the mission centre of the whole church, and therefore that anything given to that church is liable to result in blessing that will go well beyond its borders. If so, this is yet another example of the overflowingness of God's blessing.

The beautiful thought expressed in verse 14 may well have meant a great deal to Paul. He had a deep sense of the oneness of the Christian church, as the Epistle to the Ephesians and also 1 Corinthians 1-4 and 12 show to us at the universal and local levels respectively. Christian unity is not primarily organizational, but rather spiritual, and so the love that would be evoked in the hearts of the folk at Jerusalem for the Corinthian church would be a matter of real importance.

Not only so, but they would be encouraged to pray for the Corinthians. Seeing the genuineness of their faith, they would probably now labour in prayer that that faith might grow and that the church's witness in its difficult environment would be extended and blessed.

In verse 15, Paul, having written much about thanksgiving, now lifts up his own heart to God in gratitude. The grace God has given to the Corinthians and which enabled them to give, was a 'surpassing grace' (v. 14). By using this phrase, Paul may have been reminded of his own reference in 8:9 to the grace of Christ in becoming poor for our sakes. Whether this is so or not, he now moves on to write of God's indescribable gift, which is surely Christ himself.

A word like 'surpassing' suggests the straining of the limits of language, but 'indescribable' indicates that, even at the outer linguistic limits, words can never be adequate to describe the matter in hand. This is certainly true of God's gift in Christ. We can describe this great gift but never adequately; we may preach Christ, but never do him justice; most of all, we may make him the Theme of our thanksgiving, but always with a sense that this great Theme far outstrips that praise itself.

3. Concluding thoughts on 9:6-15

In recent years, teaching known as Prosperity Theology has gained ground in some circles. In its extreme form, this theology teaches that God wills material prosperity for every Christian, and that poverty is evidence of personal spiritual failure. In some ways this is similar to the view that sickness always has a particular spiritual cause in the sick person. A more moderate form teaches that we should normally expect prosperity for obedient Christians.

Is Paul teaching this doctrine here, especially in verses 6-11? On the face of it, we might think so. There are however some important considerations to be kept in view.

First of all, we should note that the teaching of these verses is very much like certain passages in the Book of Proverbs (e.g. 10:22, 'the blessing of the Lord brings wealth'). It is a characteristic of Proverbs that it sets out general principles without normally taking account of exceptions. In fact, this is a general feature of all proverbs, whether inspired or not.

Secondly, the Old Testament certainly knows of godly people who are poor (e.g. Prov. 19:1; cf. James 2:5). It is unlikely that, if Paul's teaching was meant to set out an invariable principle, it would not apply in the Old Testament also, particularly as he quotes that testament to support his thesis. The Old Testament normally presents the poor as people to be helped, not blamed.

Thirdly, what are we to make of the 'extreme poverty' of the Macedonians (8:2), whose example of generosity Paul uses as an encouragement to the Corinthians to give? If Prosperity Theology is correct, should he not rather have censured them for their poverty, or at least asked them to consider whether they were committing some sin?

Fourthly, we should note that our passage here appears in the context of an exhortation to give. Paul's great concern is not the prosperity of the Corinthians, but the relief of poverty in Jerusalem – and that poverty was real.

Finally, motivation is of great importance in Christian ethical decisions, and there is little doubt that Prosperity Theology appeals to the greed that may affect even Christians in our modern society, while in this passage the motives for giving are the blessing of others and the praise of God.

All in all, we can only assume that what Paul says here does not teach Prosperity Theology, but simply the general principle that God often gives generously to those who themselves give, but in order that they may give still more and do so to his glory.

Some questions for personal reflection:

1. In so far as I know my own heart, what are my motives in my giving?

2. Can I see the principles of sowing and reaping at work in my life?

3. What place does the glory of God have in my thinking?

4. If I had the opportunity of speaking to my church about Christian giving, what would I say?

15: CHRISTIAN CONSISTENCY (10:1-11)

Paul's letters have suffered less from those who wish to divide them up than have some of the Old Testament books. Not only so, but where this has been done, with some exceptions, the different parts are normally all attributed to Paul himself.

This second letter to the Corinthians has often been viewed by scholars as composed of parts of more than one letter from Paul to this church. Particularly, it has often been held that chapters 10-13 have come from another of Paul's letters, and possibly from the 'severe letter' he had written to them when there was so much trouble at Corinth.

This matter is dealt with fully in the Introduction,[1] but let us note, as said there, that it is a good principle to try to deal at its face value with a piece of literature that has come down to us as a unity. Only if this proves impossible, or at least very difficult, should we seek for some composite theory to account for its present literary state.

Our conviction is that this epistle does make sense in the form in which it has come down to us, and that therefore we should interpret it as it is without recourse to theories of fragmentation. Amongst other things, we will seek in the chapters that follow to show its integrity with the rest of the letter.

1. His concern (1, 2)

In New Testament Greek, a writer has several available ways of putting emphasis on the fact that it is he who is writing. Paul does this particularly strongly here. Why?

Could it be to stress that this is his own personal sentiment rather than that of Timothy, whom he associated with him in the writing of the letter (1:1)? Possibly, for he does go on to

1. See Introduction, pp. 18-21.

write of the image of him which some at least at Corinth enter-
tained. Certainly his use of the first person plural, which is fairly
common in the epistle up to this point, is much less so from
now on.

If he is excluding Timothy for the time being, he makes a
connection with Somebody incomparably greater. His reference
to Christ here makes an important link with what immediately
precedes this passage, with the close of chapter 9.

There he wrote of Christ as the incomparable gift of God.
Although indescribable in the sense that, in all his fulness, he is
completely beyond any form of literary expression, particular
attributes of Christ can be mentioned, and he does refer here to
two of these, Christ's meekness and gentleness.

Paul has had so much to say about Christian service in this
letter that it would not be surprising if he had in his mind the
picture of the supreme Servant of the Lord who appears in Isaiah,
chapters 42, 49, 50 and 52:13-53:12.

The character qualities of that Servant, who seems also to
be his model in 2 Timothy 2:24-26, are to be found in the description given in verse 1 here, as a glance at Isaiah 42:1ff. will
show. They are certainly illustrated in the story of the seizure
and trials of Christ.

Verse 2 of the NIV places 'timid' and 'bold' within quotation marks, and certainly Paul here gives every impression of
quoting things that had been said about him at Corinth. They
implied that he was really a fundamentally cowardly man who
has tried to promote an image of boldness through his letters.

Paul clearly does not accept this criticism. At the same time
it is clear that he has no desire to be bold, if this means going
into action against his critics. Such 'boldness' would give him
no pleasure. He would far rather come and find that all is well
in the church at Corinth.

In verse 2, he refers to 'some people'. This phrase is used by

those who think Paul is here writing only for the recalcitrant
minority. It needs to be pointed out, however, that, although he
refers here to some, these chapters are in fact addressed to all,
just as the remainder of the epistle is.

This vocal group apparently accused Paul of worldliness of
outlook. How strange this criticism seems when we read First
Corinthians! There he spends the first four chapters pointing
up the great contrast between worldly thinking and the wisdom
that comes from God! A great deal of the present epistle really
shows us how utterly different Paul's style of ministry was from
worldly methods of communication and of influencing others.

The words, 'according to the standards of this world', render
a phrase which, literally translated, means 'according to the
flesh'. He used this twice in 5:16 and it is clear there that it
referred to a worldly outlook, both on people in general and on
Christ in particular. Here it relates more to the lifestyle that
results from such an outlook.

2. His weapons (3-6)

These verses are completely dominated by the analogy of the
warrior. The concept of spiritual warfare is one that lies behind
a great deal of the New Testament, for Christianity came into
the world as a missionary faith, and such a faith is bound to
arouse antagonism. It still does today.

Paul recognized, as his Master also did (John 17:14-16), that
the followers of Christ have to live in the alien environment of
the world (v. 3). It is the fact that we have corporeal existence
and a social environment that provides us with a plenitude of
analogies, but we also need to be constantly aware that, despite
all the analogies between the spiritual on the one hand and the
physical and social on the other, there is a vast chasm of difference between Christianity and anything the surrounding world
affords. Paul's argument here is an interesting example of the

way in which analogy can be used to establish difference as well as similarity.

His general statement of verse 3 is given more detailed articulation in the verses that follow. First of all he writes of the weapons he uses in the spiritual struggle. He has already referred to 'weapons of righteousness in the right hand and in the left' (6:7), without specifying them. Neither does he specify them here.

Could this mean that this analogy was one he used so frequently in his ministry to believers that he did not need to be specific on every occasion? If so, this would make Ephesians 6:10-20, and especially its reference to Scripture and to prayer, especially valuable. He probably has these two weapons in view in writing the present passage.

These weapons may not seem sharp to men but in fact divine power resides in them (v. 4, cf. Rom. 1:6), and that power demolishes strongholds.

In the ancient world, much of warfare was concentrated on cities. These, with their walls, were built with possible enemy attacks in view and, if there was sufficient warning, the whole population of the villages forming a city's hinterland would crowd within these walls to find safety there. Military commanders therefore employed great battering rams to overcome these city strongholds. Paul recognized that God has his own powerful weapons against the strongholds of Satan.

Paul used the Word of God and came to God in prayer in order to demolish arguments (v. 5). It is worth noting that he did so, not only explicitly in messages like the synagogue sermon recorded in Acts 13, but also in his preaching to Gentiles, such as the Areopagus sermon of Acts 17. Here, although he does not quote from the Old Testament, all his thought is shot through with its phraseology and ideas.

The word translated 'pretension' (v. 6) means literally 'that

which is lifted up' and Paul may be here picturing the high
walls of a city. Just as Israel, following God's instructions, saw
the walls of Jericho collapse, so the Christian, using the powerful spiritual weapons God gives him, may see similar victories,
although now in the spiritual realm.

The terms, 'arguments', 'knowledge of God' and 'every
thought' suggest ideological enemies, and the church has always had these, whether in Paul's day or in later generations or
today. Paul encountered these, both among the Jews and also
the Greek philosophers, and he employed arguments, based on
the Scriptures and the gospel, to overcome them. Each of his
sermons recorded in Acts does this.

The phrase, 'knowledge of God' is not entirely intellectual,
for it implies personal acquaintance with God as well as con-
ceptual knowledge of him, but its use in a verse like this shows
that there is an intellectual side to it. The gospel is a communication of truth which is designed to give the hearer a clearer
understanding of what God is like and what his way with men
and women is.

The expressions, 'take captive' and 'obedient', may suggest
the widespread practice of enslaving defeated enemies. At the
very least, it means that the Christian preacher is concerned
that rebels against Christ should be subdued by their voluntary
surrender to him.

We might note how intimately related God and Christ are in
this verse. Clearly Paul is concerned that people should have
the knowledge of God and yet, at the same time, that they should
be obedient to Christ. If these are the intellectual and volitional
sides of the same experience, this tells us that, in Paul's mind,
Christ is God.

Paul has moved in his analogy from handling weapons to
overcoming strongholds, and now he moves on through taking
captives to punishing offenders.

He writes of the completion of obedience by the Corinthians. What does this imply? Perhaps that the offenders at the church still retained some sympathisers among the general body of the believers there, and that Paul felt the need to wait until all the main body saw the need for disciplining them.

This suggests perhaps that he saw church discipline, not as something to be simply imposed from outside, but rather something in which the local church itself must take action as one body. This appears too in 1 Corinthians 5.

Paul does not say what the punishment of the offenders would be, but it is clear that the church needed to express in some clear way its strong disapproval of what these people were doing.

3. His authority (7-11)

Paul needed at times to assert and defend the authenticity of his apostleship. He does this, for example, in his epistle to the Galatians. He makes it clear there that his gospel was under threat and that enemies in Galatia were seeking to undermine his apostleship in order to attack the gospel he preached.

Here (v. 7) he accuses the Corinthians of making superficial judgments. A reading of First Corinthians might well lead to the conclusion that they were likely to do that. Those who were enamoured by high-sounding phrases, thinking them evidence of superior wisdom (1 Cor. 1-4), and yet who could not see that tolerating serious immorality was undermining the credibility of the church (1 Cor. 5) were certainly likely to make such judgments.

They should in fact have learned this even from the Old Testament, from Samuel's words when David was selected as king in place of Saul (1 Sam. 16:7).

The expression 'belongs to Christ', used twice in verse 7, is unlikely simply to mean 'is a Christian'. It is much more likely that Paul would have used his favourite, 'in Christ', for that. Literally, the Greek phrase means 'of Christ' and probably refers to apostleship. He is not at the moment questioning the claim of the false apostles (that will come later) but rather asserting his own right to make such a claim.

In verse 8, he uses the term 'boast' which he has already employed (see 1:12 and comment there), and which he will employ extensively in the remainder of the book. A superficial reading of these chapters may give the impression that Paul was an arrogant man and that he was over-concerned about his status.

This would be a thoroughly mistaken impression. The fact that Paul's apostleship was under attack was a very serious thing. The probability is that he cared little for personal status, for he was only too well aware of his great unworthiness as a former persecutor of Christ's church. There are times though when a servant of Christ is compelled to assert the authority he has been given by Christ, not for his sake but for the gospel's.

What would we make, for instance, of a minister who, because of his faithfulness to the gospel, was told by his church that they would no longer recognize him as their minister. (It has actually happened!) Suppose he went meekly, without a word of defence? We might well come to the conclusion that he was now untrue to the gospel. Rather he should assert his gospel credentials, even if they still insist on dismissing him. We dare not deny the gospel by accepting the criticism that we do not truly represent Christ, when we know full well that we do! In such a situation it is the gospel, not our status, that is really at stake.

This then is what lies behind Paul's assertion in verse 8. The way he puts it would carry its own message to his Corinthian readers, and would perhaps remind them of 1 Corinthians 3, where he wrote of the ministries he and Apollos had exercised there, and of the good foundation he had laid in Christ and his gospel. He had also warned against building with inferior material and, most of all, against destroying the temple of God. This teaching was very relevant to what was happening in Corinth now.

There was in fact plenty of evidence that God had used him to build up the church. If the two Corinthian epistles are at all representative of his ministry there, it was certainly immensely edifying.

What though had the false apostles done? They had sown discord in the church. This was not simply building with wood, hay or stubble; it was tending towards the destruction of the temple of God.

Paul's language here is somewhat reminiscent of God's word to Jeremiah, 'See, today I appoint you over nations and kingdoms to uproot and tear down, to destroy and overthrow, to build and to plant' (Jer. 1:10). In Jeremiah's case, of course, what he had to destroy was Judah's unwarranted trust in her religious institutions (e.g. in Jer. 7) rather than in the God who gave them as means of grace, not of false confidence. In the case of the false apostles at Corinth they were pulling down a 'temple' Paul had built on the best of foundations.

In saying he is not ashamed of his authority, he uses a word from the same root as he employs in Romans 1:16. This is quite appropriate, for the apostleship he asserts here and the gospel he asserts there are intimately related to each other.

As we have already seen (vv. 1, 2), his opponents maintained that he was really like two persons, the fierce writer, the meek and mild speaker (vv. 9, 10).

His writings we know, his speaking we do not, except for the few sermons and brief addresses recorded in the Acts of the Apostles, and these are certainly well in tune with his letters. He was prepared to confront an enemy of the gospel and call

him a child of the devil (Acts 13:10), or to tell a Jewish synagogue congregation that they had judged themselves unworthy
of eternal life and that he was turning to the Gentiles (Acts
13:46). Without doubt, these men who judged so superficially
(v. 7), will have mistaken graciousness for weakness.

In response to this he says two things. First of all, he does
not want to make his letters too severe. His motive, of course,
was not to scare them, for fundamentally he was still concerned
with the building up of the church. Also he probably did not
want to give his opponents in Corinth grounds for the asser-
tions they were making about him.

Then he declares (v. 11) that when he came to Corinth, he
would act in complete accord with what he was saying here.
Let them take note of this warning!

Some questions for personal reflection:

1. Am I consistent in my character or do I vary, from bold advocate of the gospel to weak compromiser, according to my com-
pany at any one time?

2. In my Christian work, am I committed to the weapons God
has supplied, or do I use worldly methods, drawn more from
psychology, management techniques, etc. than from Scripture?

3. Do I have complete confidence in the gospel over against
any worldly philosophies I happen to know? If not, will I take
steps to build confidence through the prayerful study of God's
testimony to the gospel in the Bible?

16: GOD SETS LIMITS
TO HIS WORK (10:12-18)

Children learn a lot about life through the games they play. Some of these are devised by adults, while others are created by the children themselves. Others are so old and have been passed down through so many generations that nobody knows who first invented them.

Some of these games are competitive. Races are the most obvious example. Olympic competitors may be reasonably satisfied with a silver or a bronze medal, but no child would ever settle for one. If you are second you have lost!

Other games are co-operative. Team sports are the most obvious of these. In such games, when played in the right spirit, it is the interests of the team that matter most and the individual should take second place. Some children do not find this easy and in extreme cases never learn.

In life there is a place for both approaches and they need to be balanced. Ambition has its place, but it can get out of hand. That is why no conductor likes to have an orchestra or choir composed entirely of soloists.

When, by the grace of God, we become Christians, we begin to discover how these two principles work within the Christian church. Paul wrote to these Corinthian believers about the church as a body (1 Cor. 12), and he showed that every Christian is a member of that body, with a distinctive function. Clearly, if this is so, we need to ask God to enable us to develop the gifts he has given us.

But what is the function of these gifts? In one way, at least, it is a team function, for, as Paul says, 'The body is a unit, though it is made up of many parts; and though all its parts are many, they form one body' (1 Cor. 12:12). It is so important that, as Christians, we do not 'go it alone,' but rather seek to work together for the glory of God and the practical extension of his kingdom.

This is really what this section of Paul's letter is about. It is a practical demonstration of what can go wrong if the principles laid down in 1 Corinthians 12 are forgotten or deliberately set aside. If Paul's opponents at Corinth had read his First Epistle, they had apparently decided that chapter 12 was not for them.

1. Comparisons are odious (12)

At this point, a new note enters Paul's letter, and once it has entered it remains almost to the end. It is irony.

There is a good deal of irony in Scripture, as there is to this day in Jewish wit. Elijah's mockery of the prophets of Baal in 1 Kings 18:27 is a powerful example of it. Sometimes there is an irony within an event or a series of events that exists in historical fact before it is ever presented in written form. All four Gospel writers present the irony of the passion story, the supremely ironic event of human history. See the further comments on 11:12-33.

Paul had been dismissed as 'timid' by these opponents (v. 1). Now, with irony, he virtually admits to timidity in one area of things, for the verb translated 'dare' here is one associated with bold, brave action. He is saying that he does not have the courage to compare himself with these men. That would be altogether too bold a thing to do!

Why? They are proud men and are always blowing their own trumpets and singing their own praises, so that they are creating in the minds of others an altogether exaggerated image of themselves. Who can really compete with the person who writes false references for himself! He has probably put himself beyond competition. Having decided on such a course of action, the person concerned is more than likely to go 'over the top' and paint an excessively glowing picture of himself.

What is the implication of 12b? Is it that each of these men set himself up as a standard, and then pointed others to his own imagined virtues or gifts? This is the natural thrust of the words and may be what Paul intends his readers to understand.

On the other hand, the way he expresses his thought here could be an idiomatic way of saying that the men concerned make comparisons simply within their own circle. If they are all false then the folly of such a course of action is obvious. In terms of our illustration of the writing of references, it means that the Corinthians ought to have estimated the character of the referees as well as the value of their references. No art expert wanting to test the genuineness of an alleged Vermeer or El Greco would be so stupid as to compare it with a fake rather than with an authenticated painting by the great artist concerned.

On either interpretation, they were certainly not showing a proper humility, and this shows the aptness of his comment that they were not wise. In the opening chapters of his First Epistle to these Corinthians he made clear the nature of true wisdom, and showed that Divine wisdom cuts right across human wisdom. It is in this context, then, that, in 1 Corinthians 1:26-2:5, he underlines the fact that the servant of Christ must have due humility. True wisdom is never proud or arrogant. Note the comment on verse 17 later in this chapter.

2. Limits set (13-15a)

Because these men have discounted his own ministry, the ministry to which God had called him and which he knew he must pursue, and vaunted their own work, Paul finds it necessary to say something about himself here.

He introduces the idea of Divinely established limits for work within the Christian church (v. 13). What can this mean?

Most commentators have found the answer, probably rightly,

in Galatians 2:1-10. Paul here tells the Galatians about a meeting he and Barnabas had with the leaders of the Jerusalem church, James, Peter and John. At this meeting, these leaders, recognising the good work Paul had done among the Gentiles and the evidence of the grace of God working in that sphere of service, agreed with them on a division of labour. This was a comity agreement, in which these leaders committed themselves to the evangelization of the Jews, leaving Gentile evangelization to Paul and Barnabas. In fact it was in effect a recognition of that call to preach to the Gentiles which Paul had received at his conversion (Acts 9:15; 26:15-18).

Now if Paul's opponents at Corinth had come down from Judaea, and perhaps purported to know or even to have been sent by the leaders of the Jerusalem church, they were in fact showing that they were charlatans because of the fact that they did not recognise this comity. Paul's convictions about the importance of this principle are expanded in Romans 15:17-22, in a letter written not long after Second Corinthians.

Why was Paul so concerned about this? After all, we see from Philippians 1:12-18 that there were circumstances when he rejoiced that others were 'working his patch'. He was in prison and others were preaching the gospel openly, apparently in areas where he had formerly preached, but this caused him nothing but joy, even though he did not approve of the motivation of all of these preachers.

Not only so, but when dealing with the party-spirit at Corinth, which, among other things, produced a party which claimed allegiance to Apollos, Paul showed no concern about the influence of the other man, for he recognized him to be a true servant of God. 'I planted the seed, Apollos watered it, but God made it grow' (1 Cor. 3:6).

These two examples show that Paul's real concern was not to protect his sphere of service and to insist that it was his own private preserve. If the genuine gospel was being preached and edifying teaching being given, this gladdened his heart.

The situation at Corinth was different now, however, for the issue was not work being done by a true servant of God, like Apollos, but by opponents who were corrupting the gospel in some way (11:4, 5). They were not preaching it faithfully nor building true Christian teaching on it, and this was a serious matter.

Not only was Corinth within the field God had assigned to him, but he had actually entered that part of the field, as they well knew (v. 14). It was he who had first preached the gospel of Christ in their city, so that, humanly speaking, the Corinthian believers owed their salvation to the work done by him and the members of his evangelistic team. They could hardly deny that Corinth was within his field of service without, in so doing, denying their own salvation.

Paul goes on to say that he would not take a leaf out of his opponents' book and lay claim to work that he had not done (v. 15a). Evidently they must have been saying that the real work at Corinth had been done by them, not by Paul.

Perhaps they had claimed that the work done in the hearts of the Corinthians through Paul's ministry was incomplete and that it had to be supplemented by their own ministry to perfect it. If so, this gives them a similarity to the heretics in Galatia, who said that the gospel Paul preached had to be supplemented by the Law and circumcision. This general issue is discussed in the Introduction.[1]

There are some textual and translation problems in these verses, but they do not affect in significant measure our understanding of what Paul is saying here. The larger commentaries give details of them.

---

1. See Introduction, pp. 15, 16.

3. Evangelization expanded (15b-16)

Paul had the heart both of a pastor and of an evangelist. He had a great concern for the church at Corinth, but he also wanted to see the work of the gospel extended into other areas.

It looks as though, in the way the Holy Spirit guided the early church to a strategy of evangelism, certain cities and the churches established in them came to be seen as key centres from which the gospel might be taken to other areas. Jerusalem, where the gospel was first preached (Acts 2), and Antioch, from which all three of Paul's missionary journeys began (Acts 13:1-3; 15:35-41; 18:23), are obvious examples of this. It seems likely too that six of the seven churches of the province of Asia which are mentioned in Revelation 1-3 were evangelized from the other, the church at Ephesus.

It certainly looks as if Paul was hoping that the Corinthian church might have made a good base for further advance. A glance at its position on the map shows that, in addition to its key position as a maritime trading centre, it was the gateway to the southern part of Greece. No doubt Paul was concerned that the church there might have become so disaffected towards him and his work that it could not furnish such a base.

These verses are of great practical importance, for they pinpoint the relationship between growth in faith and evangelistic outreach. Sometimes a church's concern for the spiritual growth of its members becomes such an exclusive preoccupation that it becomes inward looking and excessively introspective, with the result that its eyes are turned away from the harvest fields outside the church. Real spiritual growth never does this. True growth in faith and concern for those outside the church to know Christ will always go hand in hand. It must do, for if we get closer to Christ we come to share his attitude to others.

Their growth in faith would expand his activity among them, for they would recognize that their faith could be strengthened and upbuilt by the kind of ministry God had given him to exercise. Those of us who have benefited so much spiritually from his epistles can readily understand this.

Because he was the apostle to the Gentiles, it was legitimate for him to seek to meet the needs of other areas further on. Whether he was thinking of the southern part of Achaia or of Italy or even of Spain (cf. Rom 15:23, 24) we do not know. It is likely, however, that the plan set out in Romans 15 was already forming in his mind.

The final sentence of verse 16 is of course a further dig at his opponents and their claims.

4. Commendation by God (17, 18)

Paul was a highly God-centred and Christ-centred man. To him the most unhappy thing about the boasting of the false apostles at Corinth was not that they denigrated his own work there, but that they drew glory away from the God who is the only true Worker in bringing people to Christ and taking them on with himself.

Just as he had done in 1 Corinthians 1:31, Paul quotes here from Jeremiah 9:24. This quotation is significant because of its context in Jeremiah, for in the first half of the chapter, the prophet is writing about his adversaries among the people of Israel, an obvious parallel to the situation in which Paul found himself in relation to the Corinthian church.

It may be then that Paul intended the Corinthians to read the verse in its context. C. H. Dodd, in his work, *According to the Scriptures*[2], contended that this intention was normal among the New Testament writers, for his thesis is that their quotations were not arbitrarily selected but were viewed as appropriate within their Old Testament contexts.

---

2. C. H. Dodd, *According to the Scriptures*, London, Nisbet, 1953.

Did he also intend they should read again that part of the First Epistle in which he had already quoted the verse from Jeremiah? Perhaps so, for the context had much to say that underlined the need for humility and also for wisdom, as we have noted in our comment on 10:12.

We should not be centred on our own service, for that makes for pride, but rather on the Lord himself (cf. 4:5-7).

The sentiment of verse 18 is obvious but it needed saying. It is often the most basic things that can be overlooked when we start moving along the wrong track in the Christian life, and a reminder of these basics never does any harm.

Some questions for personal reflection:

1. Am I guilty of measuring myself by others in my circle or even setting up my own standards for my work for the Lord, instead of accepting the standard set by Christ, God's supreme Servant?

2. Is there a place still today for recognizing that God has assigned particular spheres of service to his servants and that it is not right for us to trespass on areas assigned by him to others?

3. Is my church growing in faith in such a way that it is reaching out more and more to others with the gospel of Christ?

4. How does my answer to question 3 figure in relation to my own place as a member of that church and, like all Christians, as under the great commission to make the gospel known to others?

17: PAUL'S DEEP COMMITMENT (11:1-15)

It has been said that imitation is the sincerest form of flattery, and so it is. What it actually does is to show that the imitator recognizes the quality of what he imitates and knows that others will recognize it too.

All this is true, but of course the assumption is that the work of the imitator is actually inferior to that of the imitated, otherwise why should he not seek to promote the value of his own work? Today we have the strange situation where some imitations of the work of great and well-known artists are actually valued for themselves. This means that faking has become virtually recognized as an art-form in itself! What a strange turn-around!

There have certainly been plenty of attempts at counterfeiting the gospel, but, in the nature of the case, none of these could possibly have genuine value. Just as there is only one God and only one Christ, so there can be only one gospel. Every imitation is not simply inadequate, it is perverse, and the consequences far too great for complacency.

If you are interested in Biblical numerics, a study which has value but can be taken to excess, you will know that 7 is the perfect number. You will also know that it is not simply any lower number that expresses imperfection, but 6, and that 666 represents triple imperfection, a sinister number indeed! And why? Because, in a sense, it is trying so hard to be 7, or 777, and failing. In this realm, just to fail is to fail monumentally. Without doubt, Paul's opponents at Corinth were trying very hard, but could never succeed in being true apostles as they were fundamentally false.

Up to this point in his letter, Paul has been fairly gentle with his opponents at Corinth, but now he becomes really frank and open and designates them as servants of Satan, serving his interests and not those of the kingdom of God. The gospel they proclaim is a counterfeit and a most sinister one at that.

1. Paul the jealous 'father' (11:1-6)

Paul is obviously somewhat embarrassed by the particular line of argument in which he is forced to engage here. Self-praise is unpalatable for the Christian, and Paul shows, in what he says in 1 Timothy 1:12-17, just how deep his humility is and how great his amazement that the Lord has not only forgiven him but actually appointed him to his service. He, the proud Pharisee, has been humbled at the feet of the crucified Christ, and it is to him he wants all praise to go.

Sometimes, however, it is necessary for us to do what we find difficult and to do so in the interests of the kingdom of God. There are times, as we have noticed already, for example in 1:12ff., when a servant of Christ has to defend his ministry, because he dare not allow it to be dismissed with contempt, not for his sake but for Christ's sake. In such a situation what matters is that, whatever is said in defence of such a ministry, the one who makes the defence must preserve, or rather by God's grace be preserved in, an inward spirit of humility.

He says, 'you are already doing that,' (v. 1) because of course he has already begun to make this kind of defence earlier in the letter, as a glance at 6:3-10 and 10:12-18 will show.

Is there just a touch of playfulness in verse 1? Possibly. Some commentators have thought so. If this is so, however, in verse 2 he becomes deadly serious in what he writes.

As God reveals himself to us in the Old Testament, we find that his perfect character has many qualities. One that some readers find difficult to understand is his 'jealousy', referred to in passages like Exodus 20:5, Joshua 24:19 and Ezekiel 16:38. Here then is a quality in God which if it existed in us would call forth the divine censure, and rightly so. It is however utterly right for God to be 'jealous' when his name is defamed, his will rejected, his love spurned, his gifts attributed to gods of wood and stone. It is wrong for every possible reason for creatures God has made to turn from him and give their allegiance to worthless beings, and, moreover, it is to the eternal hurt of those who do it.

We have said that jealousy is wrong in human beings and yet Paul says here that he is jealous (v. 2). Now this too is right, for his attitude here is really a reflection of God's own attitude. Paul is not jealous for himself, but for God.

As a servant of Christ whom God has used to bring many to himself and, in fact, to establish the local church at Corinth, Paul wants to see the church there 'married' to Christ. He casts himself in the role of the father of the bride. This is a most apt illustration, for a godly father is eager for his daughter to come to her marriage as a chaste virgin and is distressed if he suspects that this is not the case.

So, as the 'father' of this church at Corinth, Paul's mind is troubled by the thought that the converts he loves so much may be diverted and defiled by some who were in fact acting for Satan (v. 3). This thought, which is certainly implied here, is spelled out explicitly later on, in verses 13-15.

In this epistle, Paul's thought has already turned to the early chapters of Genesis (cf. 4:6 and Gen. 1:3), and now he points out the parallel between Genesis 3 and the situation at Corinth. The 'serpent' who, of course, represents Satan (cf. v. 14), had spoiled God's former creation, and now he is keen to defile his new creation (cf. 5:17), the church of Christ.

Paul also refers to the deception of Eve by the serpent in 1 Timothy 2:14. He knew full well that the way to the heart is through the mind. As it was in the Garden of Eden, so it was at Corinth. Then Eve had been deceived, now the church was in danger of being led astray. That he is thinking of this as being mental deception becomes clear when we read verse 4.

Paul writes of their 'sincere and pure devotion to Christ'. This phrase testifies to his belief that their conversion had been a true one and that it had meant a wholehearted turning to Christ (cf. 1 Thess. 1:9, 10). Their devotion had been pure, for they had not tried to retain paganism at the same time as putting their trust in Christ. Whatever had happened since, there had been a decisiveness about the way they had begun with Christ.

This also shows what the real issue was in the Garden of Eden. It was not simply a matter of a piece of fruit on a tree, but whether or not there would be sincere and pure devotion to God.

The grammatical form used in verse 4 suggests that Paul is writing about something that has actually occurred. Here then is the work of the serpent in the false apostles at Corinth.

The three phrases, 'a Jesus other than', 'a different spirit', 'a different gospel', build up a very disturbing picture of preaching that was at least off centre and probably seriously heretical. These phrases employ two different words both of which are sometimes translated 'another'. The first uses the milder word *allos* but the other two the stronger word *heteros*, which means, not simply another to be added to the first but another to be distinguished from the first, different rather than additional. He uses the same two words in relation to the gospel in Galatians 1:6, 7, where the stronger is translated 'different' and the milder 'no (gospel) at all'.

Of course, Paul cannot be saying that to preach a second Jesus is legitimate, while to preach another spirit and another gospel is not, for Jesus, the spirit and the gospel are obviously closely related within the one authentic Christian message. He seems simply to be strengthening the thought of the whole sentence by his change of word. It is as if he is saying, 'an additional – no, let's rather say a counterfeit!' He does something rather similar to this in Galatians 4:9.

Verse 4 is a crucial one for identifying the nature of the outlook of Paul's opponents and commentators are divided as to their interpretation of it. In some ways it is not unlike his letter to the Galatians, especially Galatians 1:6-9. The Galatian heresy was an attempt to make Christianity a legalistic religion, to add circumcision and strenuous efforts to keep the Law to simple faith in Christ as qualifications for recognition as a Christian.

Yet it has to be said that this verse is the only evidence in the whole epistle that the 'Galatian heresy' had taken root at Corinth, and there is another possible explanation of what Paul says here. In the words of Roy Clements, 'Their error lay not in specific false teaching but in their methodology, their emphases, their leadership style. Their desire for a Christianity more congenial to the mind-set of secular Greek society demanded a gospel that majored on strength, not weakness; in heavenly triumph, not earthly suffering. In a word, they wanted a Christianity that played down the cross and played up the glory.'[1]

The virtue of this explanation is that it interprets this text in the light of the whole tenor of Paul's comments on his opponents.

In what way then was their Jesus different from Paul's? We may take our clue as to this from their whole concept of spiritual leadership, which, as we have seen, was badly wrong. It seems very likely that they had minimized the element of humility and suffering in Christ, the supreme Leader, in line with this.

If so, then, the expression 'a different gospel' is easy to understand, for the type of Jesus we believe in determines the kind of gospel we believe, and Paul's gospel undoubtedly placed great emphasis on the cross (cf. 1 Cor. 2:2).

The terms 'Jesus' and 'gospel' are of such central impor-

---

1. Roy Clements, *The Strength of Weakness*, pp. 197, 198.

tance to the Christian faith that, in line with them, we should probably understand Paul's reference to 'a different spirit' in terms of a clash of outlook concerning the Holy Spirit, the Source of the 'spirit', the inner disposition or character qualities which come from his work within the hearts of Christians. The kind of qualities these men were extolling and promoting were so different from those imparted by God's Spirit.

To whom is Paul referring as 'super-apostles' (v. 5)? Some have thought this a description of the Twelve, the phrase chosen simply because his opponents gave them an exaggerated place and contrasted Paul with them (cf. Gal. 1:6), so discounting the value of his ministry. This would fit the 'Galatian heresy' interpretation of verse 4, for it is likely that the Galatian heretics claimed to have been sent by the Jerusalem apostles.

On the other hand it makes very good sense to interpret it in the light of verse 13, and to see Paul's claim not to be inferior to them as deep irony. Of course, he was not inferior to them; how could truth be inferior to falsehood?

Verse 6 suggests that his opponents had won their way to recognition by the Corinthians in view of their verbal eloquence, for training in rhetoric was highly regarded in the Greek world of the day. Paul had apparently never had formal rhetoric in his education.

What he had however was far more important. It was knowledge and understanding of the gospel facts. His speaking may not have been brilliant but it was squarely founded on truth, and this is infinitely more important.

Two Christian friends of mine once went to hear a well-known speaker. Robert was very impressed by the man's oratory but felt vaguely uncomfortable. 'What do you think was wrong with that man's sermon, Alec?' he asked. The reply came swiftly and bluntly: 'There was no Jesus in it!'

Paul now moves from 'I' to 'we', for his knowledge of the

authentic gospel was shared by Timothy, whom Paul associates with himself in the opening greeting of this letter (1:1).

2. Paul the 'amateur' evangelist (11:7-12)

We can only identify the outlook of his opponents by reading 'between the lines' of Paul's letters, but this is fairly simple at this point.

It seems clear that they despised Paul for taking no fee for his gospel preaching (v. 7). If they were trained in rhetoric (v. 6), they probably insisted on being paid the 'going rate' for public speakers.

Paul had already written to the Corinthians on this subject, in 1 Corinthians 9:6-14. There he had made it clear that apostles had a right to remuneration, but that they also had the privilege of refusing it for the gospel's sake. It was this latter course Paul had taken at Corinth.

He says that he lowered himself. This was probably what his opponents found so objectionable. He had given a model of Christian leadership so different from their own that it was in fact a challenge to their genuineness, and one that all could see. Their only course then was actually to draw attention to it but to put on it their own interpretation. If he charged no fee, they said, it was clearly because he knew he was not an apostle and so did not have an apostle's rights.

The gospel had in fact elevated the Corinthians. It always does, for it is the image of God in people that imparts true dignity to them, and to re-create sinners after the image of Christ through the gospel cannot but elevate them.

Verse 8 shows that Paul had in fact received money for his gospel-preaching, not from those to whom the gospel was addressed, but from churches already established and which shared his evangelistic passion for those who did not know Christ. We can infer from Luke's account of Paul's initial visit to Corinth

that money from Philippi (Phil. 4:15) and probably from elsewhere had arrived during the course of it (Acts 18:3, 5).

It is obvious that 'robbed' was not intended literally, but rather
reflected Paul's knowledge as to how sacrificial the Macedonian Christians had been in their support of him (see next verse),
for they were so poor (cf. 8:2).

In this context, the word 'burden' means 'financial burden'.
This verse, although part of Paul's defence of himself against
criticism, is also valuable as throwing light on God's providential dealings with him. Financial support came as the need arose.

Paul shows too that he has no intention of abandoning his
policy in the light of criticism. His convictions about what his
lifestyle as an apostle should be were too deep-rooted and fundamentally Christian for that.

Verse 10 represents a forceful underlining of this. 'As surely
as the truth of Christ is in me' probably has double significance. His concern about this matter was due to the fact that he
was commissioned in the gospel to proclaim the truth of Christ,
and God's work within him had given him a concern always to
tell the truth, in this matter as in all others (cf. 1:17; 4:2, 3). The
truth we preach should in fact enter and shape our characters.

Paul's reference to 'the regions of Achaia' may suggest that
his opponents had an influence that went beyond Corinth, the
provincial capital, into other parts of Achaia. We know that there
were churches elsewhere in the province (1:1, cf. the reference
to Cenchrea, Corinth's port, in Rom. 16:1).

Verse 11 seems strange, and yet a knowledge of human nature helps us here. It is a known fact that we often like people
for whom we do something much better than those who do things
for us. The truth is that in our pride we do not like to be put in
debt to others but rather to put them in debt to us. Clearly Paul's
refusal of aid from the Corinthians had been misinterpreted by
them.

Verse 12 shows that Paul knew full well that in fact his practice was a much stronger argument for his own authenticity than his opponents were prepared to admit.

3. The false apostles (11:13-15)

In these verses, Paul is at his frankest. The Corinthians must be under no illusions as to the real character of these men who were opposing his ministry.

It is doubtful whether a writer using the Greek language could make his thought more emphatic than Paul does here. Gone is the irony, even, at times possibly playfulness (see the comment on 11:1). He is now totally literal, totally serious, fiercely emphatic.

The term 'false apostles' (v. 13) is given more strength by the fact that Paul, instead of using an adjective and a noun, joins the two into one Greek word, one noun (cf. 11:26, where the same phenomenon occurs in 'false brothers'), in this way implying that their 'apostleship' and their 'falseness' were inseparable. There was no way the two elements could be separated. Their whole 'ministry' was based on a lie.

To strengthen this thought still further he says they are 'deceitful workmen,' for they were not making an honest mistake but indulging in a fully culpable deception. Then, both in verses 13 and 14, he employs a word which refers to a change in the appearance of something or somebody. They were clearly pretending to be what they were not, just as Satan pretends to be an angel of light.

This last expression may well derive from the words of Christ in Luke 11:18, 'I saw Satan fall as lightning from heaven', and some have seen in it also an implied reference to the fall from heaven of the 'morning star, son of the dawn' in Isaiah 14:12, on the assumption that the king of Babylon, addressed in that passage, is a kind of grim type of which Satan is the antitype.

What is certain is that there is nothing more dangerous than darkness presenting itself as light, and, as the deceiver, Satan is a master of that.

To put the matter totally beyond doubt, in verse 15, Paul identifies these men as servants of Satan. His closing words are sombre in their implication of Divine judgment for them.

Some questions for personal reflection:

1. If I have led people to Christ, do I feel the same 'godly jealousy' for their pure devotion to Christ that Paul showed for the people he loved in Corinth?

2. What features in the picture of Jesus given in the Gospels are sometimes played down, and what are the dangers of this?

3. When listening to preachers, what do I tend to regard the more highly, the content of their messages or the style of their communication? What does my answer tell me about myself?

4. What may the church today learn from what Paul says about freely preaching the gospel but being willing to receive money from Christians for his work? Can this be applied today? If so, how?

18: PAUL'S CONSTANT SUFFERINGS (11:16-33)

Irony would hardly exist in a perfect world. This does not by any means imply that its use is illegitimate in an imperfect one.

The whole point of irony, of course, is that, either in word or deed, there is a presentation of truth in terms of its opposite. Like paradox, which G. K. Chesterton described as truth standing on its head to attract attention, verbal irony can be a powerful communication tool when wisely and not unkindly used.

In the drama of the crucifixion, history's greatest irony was played out. The enemies of Jesus put on his head a crown of thorns and around his shoulders they draped a brilliantly coloured robe. They gave him as throne a cross and taunted him with being Son of God, Saviour of others, and King of Israel.

Their actions were intended to be ironic, for they did not accept his kingship. Yet, by a supreme Divine irony, we might almost call it a counter-irony, their ascriptions to him of Kingship, Saviourhood and Divine Sonship could not have been more appropriate. In fact, it is because of the cross that he reigns now in the hearts of so many and will be seen ultimately to reign over the whole world.

Paul served this crucified Christ and we see elsewhere, notably in Romans 6, that he regarded the cross, not only as God's way of saving men and women, but also as a pattern for Christian discipleship. It would not be surprising therefore if we found that there was a repetition or at least some reflection of the irony of the cross in the experience of the followers of Christ, Paul included. Just as Christ was himself discounted, persecuted and shamed by man and yet vindicated by God, so we might expect this to be true of his servants.

This is in fact what we do find here, and it is perhaps particularly appropriate that Paul should give written expression to it by the use of verbal irony, which he does here.

1. His foolishness – and theirs (11:16-21a)

It is a kind of irony when, in his Corinthian correspondence, Paul sometimes describes himself as a fool. He does so in First Corinthians in a discussion of the radical difference between godly wisdom and the wisdom of the world. There he says that what the world regards as wise is really foolishness but that the message of the cross, dismissed contemptuously as utter folly, is actually the supreme expression of the wisdom of God (1 Cor. 1:18-25). Then in 1 Corinthians 3:18-20 he says that we have to become 'fools' by abandoning the world's wisdom for God's, and then declares that he and his fellow-apostles have become fools for Christ's sake (1 Cor. 4:9-14), because they are prepared to be regarded as the scum of the earth for the sake of Christ.

His thought here is somewhat different from what he wrote in his First Epistle. It is really a kind of role-play. Just as an actor may play a part which is alien to his character and convey a message through this, so Paul makes his point through this alien role. The prophet Zechariah had been told by God to do something like this, when he acted out two parts, that of a good and that of a worthless shepherd (Zech. 11:4-17).

Paul has to risk actually being taken for a fool, even by brothers in Christ, in order to make his point in relation to the false apostles and their claims. Even if they misunderstand him and take him for an actual fool, he is still prepared to take the line on which he has determined, because he must. It involves playing the part of a boaster, in imitation of the boasting of his opponents.

He says (v. 17), 'In this self-confident boasting I am not talking as the Lord would, but as a fool.' 'The Lord' here seems to mean, not simply God but 'the Lord Jesus', rather in the way Paul uses this expression in 1 Corinthians 7:10, 12, 25. As we can see by reading the Gospels, Jesus did not in fact take this path in any of his encounters with his enemies. Paul has already referred to the meekness and gentleness of Christ (10:1). If he is departing from this model, however, it is as a ploy, a stratagem, not because he finds boasting palatable. If it were real boasting, it would be quite alien to the spirit of Christ, but it is not.

His opponents had followed the world's way in their boasting (v. 18), and so he will do so too. The real difference between him and them was of course in motivation.

Commenting on verses 19-21a, Murray Harris says, 'Probably no verses in the epistle are more scathingly ironical than these.'[1] The Corinthians, as we may infer from 1 Corinthians 3:18-21, tended to rate worldly wisdom much too highly. Well then, Paul implies, if they really do reckon themselves wise, how supremely foolish they must be to put up with what they have had to suffer at the hands of the false apostles.

Verse 20 is most revealing. It opens to us a picture of false teachers of a most arrogant kind, lording it over the church at Corinth, just as Diotrephes did over the church to which the apostle John was later to write (3 John 9, 10). They had really treated the Corinthian believers like dirt, and yet, incredibly, they had taken it!

How ironic is verse 21a! These false apostles gloried in their power. As 'apostles of Christ' they threw their weight about and they did so in a most obnoxious fashion. 'They reckon I am weak?' asks Paul. 'Why, yes, so I am! If power is to be identified by this sort of conduct, then put my name down – and Timothy's name ('we', cf. 1:1) – as those of weak men!'

---

1. Murray Harris, '2 Corinthians' in F.E. Gaebelein (ed.), *Expositor's Bible Commentary*, Vol. 10, Grand Rapids, Zondervan, 1976, *ad loc.*

2. His sufferings (11:21b-29)

Paul's reluctance to boast is shown in the fact that he has deferred it to this point in his letter.

At first he refers simply to qualifications which he and they possess together (vv. 21b, 22). In these respects they are on an equal footing.

The three expressions he uses in verse 22 may seem like synonyms, but in fact they are not.

'Hebrews' is a linguistic and cultural term. Paul had been reared with the language and with the culture that obtained within the Holy Land itself, not that of Hellenistic Judaism. This does not mean that he was born in the Holy Land, nor that he did not know Greek, for clearly he did, but rather that he was 'a Hebrew of the Hebrews' (cf. Phil. 3:5), speaking the language and reared in the culture of the land, even though born outside it.

'Israelites' is probably here a racial term, denoting the descendants of Jacob, members of the twelve tribes of Israel.

'Abraham's descendants' had rather fuller implications, for the great covenant promises God made to Israel were first made to Abraham (Gen. 12:1f.), so it was a claim to stand within the great Old Covenant purpose of God and to inherit its promises.

So then if language, culture, race and religious inheritance meant anything, Paul and these men were equal. This certainly establishes beyond doubt that they were Jews.

It is in verse 23 that he begins to assert superiority, and so says not simply that he is a fool but that he is going beyond folly into madness. His claims are however strikingly paradoxical.

We are perhaps so used to this great passage that we do not realize how singular it really is. In fact, the real basis of discerning its meaning is an understanding of the gospel itself, for this is centred in One who himself faced every manner of suffering and shame because of his commitment to the will of God. Such a concept of 'greatness' was utterly new to the world, and to the Hellenistic world occupied by the Corinthians perhaps most of all. Like all Greeks, the people of Corinth would rate certain human qualities very highly and physical perfection was one of these. A Man impaled on a rough tree and with nails through his hands and feet would possess little attraction for them.

It is probable that these false apostles had majored on qualifications, and had recited them to the Corinthians on their arrival at their church, and, when they felt the time was ripe, tried to show that Paul's were inferior to theirs. His qualifications as a servant of Christ were however greater than theirs.

Much of this catalogue of sufferings can be independently verified from the Acts of the Apostles and we will indicate points of correspondence whenever possible. It is important, of course, to remember that the purpose of Luke's account of the early church is not to show the sufferings of Paul but the progress of the gospel. When this is taken into consideration, it is remarkable how much verification there is.

Of course, we know nothing of any sufferings experienced by the false apostles, but, if they really were as studiously false as Paul says they were, we can be sure that they would avoid suffering whenever it was possible to do so.

This moving account of his trials for the sake of Christ, commences with the simple statement, 'I have worked much harder' (v. 23). Luke tells us that Paul worked at his trade of tent-making (Acts 18:3; 20:34) as well as his gospel preaching and pastoral care for the churches, and Paul alludes to this work elsewhere (1 Cor. 4:12; 1 Thess. 2:9; 2 Thess. 3:8). The fact that he began with this comparatively modest claim may itself point to his reluctance to write in the way he is now doing.

We know of his imprisonment at Philippi (Acts 16:22-40),

and there was, of course, to be more experience of prison to come subsequent to his writing of this letter. It has sometimes been assumed that he had a period of imprisonment at Ephesus.

His experiences of flogging (v. 23; cf. Acts 16:22, 23) and lashing by the Jewish authorities (v. 24) must have been terrible to experience. Probably when enduring these he would remember the dreadful flogging his Lord experienced at the hands of the Romans shortly before his death. The Jews were not allowed to exceed forty strokes in flogging (cf. Deut. 25:1-3) and they deliberately numbered them short of this in case of mistakes.

Beating with rods (v. 25) was a Roman punishment and Roman citizens were specifically excluded from it. Paul's words recorded in Acts 16:37 may suggest therefore that this was the completely illegal punishment he and Silas received at Philippi. This was evidently not an isolated case. Luke records a stoning in Acts 14:19.

We know of course of Paul's experiences at sea at a later time, but not of the things he mentions here. Until his last journey to Rome, most of his sea journeys will probably have been short, but several would be hazardous, traversing rough waters.

Verse 26 covers a great deal of ground, and Paul probably ended it with 'danger from false brothers' because of possible parallels with the situation he was now dealing with at Corinth.

Verse 27 brings together a number of experiences which would take their toll of Paul's physical constitution.

Verse 28 startles us. It is so different from all that has gone before it. Perhaps too our own concern is too shallow to realize that for Paul concern for all the churches was actually painful. He loved those he had led to Christ, and he felt under great pressure from concern for them. Of course that concern would be translated into letter-writing and where possible into action, but there were limits to what he could do personally. After all, he could only be in one place at a time. He could however pray and his letters, specially their opening and concluding sections, show how much he did this.

This concern was a daily one for Paul. Some of his other sufferings, intense as many of them were, would not have been long-lasting, but there was no remittance from this.

What does verse 29 mean? There are two main interpretations. Is Paul saying that he, Christ's apostle, is himself weak, and that the weakness and tendency to temptation that others feel, he is also aware of? In other words, is he really reminding them that he, who from one point of view can be thought of as Christ's under-shepherd, is, from another point of view, simply a frail and failing sheep?

This would make good sense, but it is more likely that he is here developing the thought of verse 28 and describing his deep sense of identification with the churches in all their frailty and liability to sin.

3. His weakness (11:30-33)

The way Paul puts his thought in verse 30 shows that he was under some definite constraint. He *must* boast (cf. 12:1). This constraint may have come from within, from a sense that this was what the occasion required. On the other hand, it may have been external, for there may well have been some at Corinth who were demanding that he produce his credentials. If we had nothing more than this, we could not have been sure which he meant, but what he says in 12:11 (see the comment there) makes it seem highly likely that the constraint was an outward one, arising from the Corinthians themselves.

This verse also sums up the nature of the events and factors in his life of which Paul has been 'boasting' in the last few verses. In fact, they are evidence, not of his powerful personality or towering gifts, the kind of evidence to which the false apostles would probably have pointed in their own case, but rather of his human frailty. They therefore witnessed to the fact that God was at work in him. Would anybody but a true servant of Christ have been willing to endure such things, at so many levels of suffering, so frequently and in such a sustained way? And who but one who was upheld by a strength not his own, a Divine strength, could have lasted the course?

The list is so extensive and the sufferings so great that Paul feels it necessary to appeal to the fact of God's all-seeing knowledge for support (v. 31), in case his readers think he is exaggerating. We cannot be sure whether the words, 'who is to be praised for ever', refer to 'the God and Father' or to 'the Lord Jesus'. This is rather a similar situation to that we find in Romans 9:5, although there the greater likelihood is that the words apply to Christ while here to God.

There are times when a communication becomes so solemn and its emotional impact so intense that the speaker or writer feels it wise to lighten it briefly. Perhaps this is what Paul is doing here, for he is now introducing, right at the end of his account of his sufferings, almost as an afterthought, a story with a humorous touch to it.

The incident to which he refers is recorded by Luke in Acts 9:23-25. There are some differences between that account and what Paul says here, but these differences are not of a character to render them incompatible. There is no unlikelihood in a situation where both Jews and the governor responsible to King Aretas were concerned to capture Paul, for Aretas the king of the Arab kingdom of Nabataea, a vassal of Rome, was related by marriage to the Herod family, which had played an important part in governing the Jews.

Here, perhaps somewhat with tongue in cheek, Paul is making the point that he, the apostle of the Gentiles, had been prepared to suffer the indignity of such a descent from a city wall.

How would the false apostles, with their arrogance and delusions of spiritual grandeur, have taken to that? It is perhaps his way of saying that he was prepared for loss of dignity as well as physical sufferings in the service of Christ.

Whatever the point here, we should note that Paul received not only inner strength to face suffering but also outward protection from capture, so that he might continue his work for the Lord.

Some questions for personal reflection:

1. Do I still retain in my mind some worldly criteria for estimating the authenticity of a servant of Christ and the value of such a person's work for the Lord?

2. What do any inconveniences I may have had as the cost of my witness for Christ look like in comparison with what Paul had faced?

3. How deep is my concern for the church to which I belong?

4. Do I feel that some things I may need to do in Christ's service are really below my dignity? If so, what does that tell me about myself?

19: REALLY AN APOSTLE? (12:1-13)

Many people have had experiences in life about which they are reluctant to talk.

Some of these are skeletons in the cupboard. At some time or other they have done something of which they are now thoroughly ashamed. They look back on it with great distaste and they could never be induced to make it a topic of conversation. In some cases it might even have been an illegal act and they are afraid, not only of the opinion of their friends, but also of the arm of the law.

There are others who will not talk about something in the past for a completely different reason. The experience was so wonderful that they feel quite unable to communicate it. Perhaps they feel they can never really express it in such a way as to convey to others what happened. They may even feel that to verbalize it at all is to risk trivializing it.

Some Christians feel like this about their conversion experience, but in fact it is right, indeed vital, for us to be prepared to give a verbal witness to what Christ has done in our lives, so long as we place him, and not ourselves, at the centre of what we say.

We should note carefully that in this passage it is not his conversion Paul is writing about. We have the record from Luke of two occasions when Paul spoke very clearly about this (in Acts 22 and 26) and there are other passages where he makes at least a brief allusion to it (e.g. in Gal. 1:13-16; 1 Tim. 1:13, 14).

What was it then that happened to Paul and that he was reluctant to talk about? It is time we looked at the passage itself.

1. A special experience (12:1-6)
Paul's language in verse 1 repeats what he has said in 11:30 (see the comment there), and shows that in what he says he is

still under some kind of constraint, either internal or external. The balance of probability would certainly seem to be towards external constraint, for he says there is nothing to be gained by it.

It may well be that the false apostles had made much of certain visions and direct revelations they claimed to have had from God, and used these in their claim to be authentic servants of Christ. The term 'revelation' is wider and less specific than 'vision', which clearly implies some visual experience. Cults and heresies have often specialized in this kind of thing, although this is not to say that every experience of this sort is counterfeit, as the apostle's own testimony makes clear to us.

At verse 2, Paul alters his way of writing. In fiction, an author may assume the viewpoint of one of his characters and tell a story as through his or her eyes. On the other hand he may take a position above the whole story and tell it in the third person. Paul, dealing of course with truth and not fiction, takes a different writing stance from what he has done before. Having written about his own experiences, he now goes on to describe somebody else's. At least, that is what he appears to be doing – but things are not always what they seem!

'A man in Christ' is, of course, simply a Christian, but a Christian considered from the standpoint of his union with Christ, for that is the meaning of the phrase, 'in Christ'. Paul's choice of this way of describing a Christian was probably due to the fact that he was writing about a mystical experience, and the language of spiritual union is obviously appropriate for that.

As we will soon see, Paul was actually writing about himself. The experience was a long time ago. His reference to fourteen years takes us back to a period in his life of which Luke says nothing in Acts, except for the bare fact that he was in his home city of Tarsus (cf. Acts 9:30; 11:25).

This man was 'caught up to the third heaven'. Was this a

physical or a spiritual experience? Luke uses the same verb in Acts 8:39 in relation to an experience of Philip the evangelist, a clearly physical experience. Paul was unable himself to say what had actually happened in his case. Probably the experience was so vivid that he was quite unconscious of himself while it was going on. If it will be like that in heaven, what a blessing to be rid of self-preoccupation!

What does he mean by 'the third heaven'? In New Testament times, some Jewish thought distinguished between the first, the lower visible heaven, where the birds fly, the second, the upper visible heaven, where the heavenly bodies are, and the third heaven, the very abode of God himself. Paul is therefore using Judaism's conventional language here.

Verse 4 commences with a re-statement of the thought of verse 3. The unusual nature of the experience perhaps accounts for the repetition, but Paul now adds the words, 'God knows', surely to discourage speculation on the part of his readers. Let it be enough, he suggests, that God knows.

Here he identifies the 'third heaven' of verse 3 with 'paradise'. This word came into Hebrew, Aramaic and Greek as a loan-word from the ancient Persian language. Originally it simply meant 'park' or 'walled garden'. In course of time it came to be used by the Jews of a place with idyllic conditions of life, and so was applied both to the Garden of Eden and to the future Messianic kingdom, Eden restored. Between the past and the future was the present, the hidden Paradise, as they called it, where the disembodied spirits of Abraham and his fellow patriarchs dwelt in bliss.

What Paul says here shows indirectly, but clearly, that he believed the disembodied state to be not only one of bliss, but of bliss in the presence of God. This certainly harmonizes well with what he says about being, after death, 'at home with the Lord' (5:8; cf. Phil. 1:23).

The things Paul heard while in paradise were inexpressible, probably both in the sense that human language was not fitted to convey them and also that he was not permitted to do so, although, of course, it is the latter that is emphasized in the remainder of his sentence.

The word 'man' here suggests Paul was taking into account the fact that others may have had somewhat similar experiences and were likewise banned from communicating their content. Deuteronomy 29:29 distinguishes between the secret things that belong to the Lord and those that are revealed for our learning and our doing.

From verse 5 to verse 7 he gradually shows us that he is actually writing about himself. The strange way in which this comes out into the open reveals the kind of embarrassment that may cause someone to proceed to clear statement by way of preliminary circumlocution.

Why was Paul embarrassed? We can see the reason in verse 5.

The experience itself had been a wonderful one, and, of course, it was given because he was 'in Christ' (v. 2). From one angle, therefore, he saw that he could indeed 'boast' about such experiences entirely without pride, because he knew full well that his very standing in Christ was not due to any merit of his own but was entirely due to the grace of God. Hence, this must be true of an experience like this, which was the fruit of that gracious standing.

So far, so good. But, because he knew of his personal unworthiness, he could not avoid feeling he did not want to talk about such things, in case people thought he was claiming to be somebody special.

So, the distinction between 'a man like that' and 'myself' is the distinction between Paul as placed 'in Christ' by God's grace, and Paul considered in himself, an unworthy servant of Christ. One with Christ and exalted with him, and yet also a servant of

Christ, humbled before him – that is the paradox which lies behind Paul's thought here.

It is because of his sense of unworthiness then that Paul, in outlining his 'qualifications', majors on his weaknesses, as he did, of course, in the previous chapter, although he indicates in the next verse that he was in fact telling the truth in what he had just said.

Verse 5 shows too that he had made a conscious choice not, in the normal course of things, to say anything about such experiences. It was only the special constraint under which he was writing that had caused him to tell it now. In fact, he wished to be judged by others on the basis of his deeds and words, not his private experiences. He knew full well that such experiences were no ground whatever for boasting by a man all too conscious of his weaknesses. He had, of course, made it clear earlier in this same letter that his great desire in his ministry was to exalt Christ and not himself (4:5ff.).

2. A sore trial (12:7-10)

These verses are intimately linked with the previous section, for Paul is here writing about the aftermath of his visionary experience. It is most important to note too that, having reluctantly implied in verse 6 that the visionary in verses 2 to 4 was himself, he says so really plainly for the first time in verse 7. Why is it noteworthy? Because it is just at the point that he begins to write again about his weaknesses.

In verse 6 he says he does not want people to think more highly of him than is warranted, and then in verse 7 he shows that God's concern was that he should not think too highly of himself.

This verse is remarkably helpful in its balance, and for the way it relates and yet distinguishes the activity of God and that of Satan.

Paul writes here of a distressing element in his experience and interprets it in two apparently contradictory and yet actually complementary ways. The distressing element is described as 'a thorn in the flesh'. The simple but eloquent image of some kind of festering splinter is, of course, familiar to us all. What did he mean by it?

Was it an illness? This is the view of many, perhaps of most, modern commentators, and support for this has been found from a passage like Galatians 4:13, 14. Certainly fine Christian people have prayed for God to remove a chronic illness and instead have been given grace to bear it.

Yet it is a good principle of Biblical interpretation to seek light from the Old Testament on the meaning of a New Testament passage that is difficult to understand. So some commentators, both ancient and modern, have followed the great fourth century preacher, John Chrysostom, in finding a clue to Paul's meaning in Numbers 33:55 (cf. Jud. 2:3; Ezek. 28:24). There God describes the enemies that would be left in the land of Israel as thorns in the sides of his people, and in Ezekiel 2:6 it is the enemies of the prophet among the actual people of Israel who are cast in this role.

How appropriate such a background would be to the actual circumstances of Paul's life, of which the Corinthian Christians were only too aware! He had been dogged by enemies wherever he went, and some of them were within the actual fold of the church, such as the false apostles at Corinth. It would not be surprising if he had asked the Lord for deliverance from them.

What was the source of this thorn? Paul calls it a messenger of Satan and it was obviously frustrating for him. The expression is appropriate too, whether the thorn should be thought of as illness or enemies, because Genesis shows us both physical imperfections in the world and human enmity against the purpose of God arriving on the earthly scene as consequences of *as Satan had "purpose*

Satan's successful temptation of Adam and Eve (Gen. 3:14-19; 4:3-12). Clearly Satan's purpose in the thorn was a negative one, to torment Paul.

But God also had a purpose in it, and this was to prevent Paul from being conceited. In fact, the expression, 'there was given me,' must imply that God was its source. After all, we can hardly imagine Satan seeking to make Paul humble, in other words to make him more like Christ!

paradox This means, then, that we face a kind of paradox here. But this is in fact a paradox within our own experience too. Christians in general recognize the overall sovereignty and loving purpose of God, but we are also aware of the malign designs of Satan.

What Paul did was perfectly natural: he asked the Lord to take the thorn away. None of us takes kindly to the presence either of enemies or of sickness and there is nothing wrong with praying for their removal.

God did not however remove the thorn. It is worth noting now what Paul did not do. There is no suggestion that he asked himself if he was lacking in faith. Of course, sometimes there is a lack of faith in our praying, but this was not the case here. It does show, however, that there is a place for accepting what comes to us under the overall sovereignty of God. *enemies*

He prayed three times, perhaps following the example of Christ in Gethsemane (Mark 14:32-42). If Paul's thorn was his enemies, there is a parallel here, for Christ was about to suffer deeply at the hands of his enemies, although of course with a profound Divine purpose in that he was suffering for our sins.

There is another parallel too. Luke tells us (Luke 22:43) that the Father sent an angel to strengthen his Son. That this was no special enabling denied to us is clear from the fact that an assurance was given to Paul too that God's strength would be given to bear this affliction.

Verse 9a follows the pattern known as 'identical parallelism' which is so common in Hebrew poetry and which must have been a natural linguistic rhythm for a Jew like Paul. This means that 'grace' and 'power' are here treated as virtual synonyms. So, in Christian use, 'grace' came to be not only the attitude of God in accepting sinners for Christ's sake apart from their merit, but, as an extension of this, God's power operating in blessing within their hearts.

Paul had learned such an important lesson from this that he had come to recognize that weakness was an opportunity to prove the power of Christ (vv. 9, 10).

His words 'for Christ's sake' perhaps indicate that he wants to distinguish between problems that may be his own fault and those that are undertaken in commitment to his vocation to spread the gospel of Christ.

The two general words, 'weaknesses' and 'difficulties', form a frame for three other expressions, 'insults', 'hardships', 'persecutions' which would certainly be appropriate if the thorn was the enemies and other afflictions he encountered in his service for Christ. See the comment on verse 7.

The final sentence of verse 10 looks like a kind of motto, summing up what Paul had found in experience and the attitude to which he had been brought. It eloquently expresses the paradox of the Christian's experience in his service for Christ.

3. Outward signs and inward character (12:11-13)

Verse 11 lends some support to the idea that Paul was being asked for credentials by critics at Corinth. He says they had driven him to talk about himself, and it is most natural to assume therefore that he wrote as he did in response to some pressure from them to do so.

His further statement that he should have been commended by them suggests that the false apostles were behind this pres-

sure to write about himself and that it was because of their in-
sinuations about him that he was having to do this. He found it
difficult to believe that the Corinthian believers, who should
have been supporting him, were actually requiring something
like this from him. See the comment on Paul's reference to letters of commendation at the start of chapter 3.

For the 'super-apostles' see the comment on 11:5.

In verse 12, Paul makes his final reference to his qualifications for apostleship. It is interesting that his reference to signs,
wonders and miracles comes right at the end of his argument.
Here he brings together three words which probably refer to the
same phenomena, but from different points of view, but we note
that he gives no examples and that he links this whole matter
with a moral quality, perseverance.

A 'sign' is a miracle from the standpoint of its significance,
the way that it points beyond itself. John's Gospel is largely a
Gospel of signs (John 20:30, 31), and the miracles of our Lord
presented there have their chief importance for John because of
the testimony they give to the Divine Sonship of Jesus.

Then Paul writes of 'wonders'. These are miracles viewed
in terms of the impression they make on the observer – he is
awestruck by them, they amaze him. Here our chief witness is
the Acts of the Apostles, for there are numerous references to
the amazement of the crowd at what God was doing through
the gospel and the miracles that accompanied its preaching (e.g.
Acts 2:12; 3:10; 13:11,12).

Finally there is the word 'miracles', and this simply means
'powers'. A miracle was an act of Divine power.

The word *semeion* ('sign') occurs twice in the verse, for the
phrase, 'the things that mark an apostle', means quite literally,
'the signs of an apostle'. Paul is therefore suggesting that the
ministry of the apostles was validated by God through miracles.

Conflicting conclusions have been drawn from this. Some maintain that the only genuine miracles after the ministry of Christ were those done by God through apostles or in their presence, i.e. the miracles that are recorded in Acts, while others have concluded that miracles are the validation of all genuine ministries.

Both views build too high a theological edifice on this verse. Paul makes this comment at a very late stage in his defence of his apostleship and he does not amplify or illustrate it. He is probably simply indicating that the God who called him to be an apostle and to preach the gospel also gave external attestation. That miracles ceased after the apostolic age, on the one hand, or that every form of ministry must be authenticated by them, on the other, are equally improbable inferences from the verse.

There was a moral quality associated with these miracles, the quality of perseverance or patient endurance. The miracles were not the easy solution to every problem, like a kind of *deus ex machina* for extricating Paul from difficulties, any more than Christ used his miraculous powers in Gethsemane's garden to avoid arrest. The very word 'perseverance' implies the presence of difficulties which need to be overcome.

What he says in verse 13 suggests that another criticism had been made of him at Corinth, probably based on his failure to arrive as previously arranged (1:15-2:1). It was being said that he was putting other churches ahead of them by continuing to serve them instead of coming to Corinth as promised.

Yet he had worked for them at Corinth without any charge, and this was evidence of genuine concern for them. With irony, he asks forgiveness for not charging them for his services to them (cf. 11:7; 1 Cor. 9:12,18)!

Some questions for personal reflection:

1. Are there any God-given experiences in my life which, although wonderful to me, could get out of proportion in my thinking about the spiritual life?

2. Have I really learned that it is when I am weak that I am strong?

3. Miracles or Christian character – which do I treat as the more important?

20: HIS PLANS TO RETURN TO THEM (12:14-13:10)

From time to time in the history of the Christian church there has been a call for reform. This has often taken the form of a desire to return to the New Testament and to see churches being modelled on what we find there.

There is something wholesome about this, for, sin being what it is, and Satan being what he is, the church is always in peril of corruption and deterioration. Nevertheless we have to think through carefully what we mean if we say that we should return to the New Testament church, to be a truly New Testament church. For we need to ask, 'Which church?' Should we model ourselves on the Jerusalem church, the Thessalonian church, the Corinthian church?

We have probably read enough in this epistle, and especially since the start of chapter 10, to make us realize that if the Corinthian church could, in some ways, furnish a model for us, in other ways it provides us with a warning.

In fact, the call to return to the New Testament must focus on the teaching the churches received rather than the imperfect response they gave to that teaching. The norm is to be found in what the apostles, commissioned by Christ to establish churches and to teach them his truth, communicated to them. Like the Corinthian church itself, we need to take seriously what Paul has said to them in this letter.

This distinction between perfect norm and imperfect expression comes out particularly strongly in our present passage.

1. His fatherly love for them (12:14-18)

The church-planting strategy of Paul often involved, not simply an initial visit to a place to preach the gospel and to establish a local church, but also subsequent personal visits, visits by other members of his team, and sometimes letters as well.

It was now something like six years since he had first come to Corinth with the gospel,[1] and he had already paid them a second visit – one which was unpleasant both for him and for them (1:23-2:1). Now he was about to come a third time (v. 14).

For the implications of the word 'burden', see the comment on 11:9. Paul is not coming to receive but to give. This was his thought too in writing a little later to the Roman church (Rom. 1:11-14). He was essentially a giver.

He wanted the Corinthians, not their possessions. This suggests an eagerness for fellowship with those it had been his privilege to lead to Christ. This kind of longing can also be seen in 1 Thessalonians 2:17-20. It is in fact natural for a Christian to thirst for fellowship, especially with those he has known and loved in the Lord, as Christ's own example makes clear to us (Matt. 26:40).

Paul saw his relationship to the Corinthian church as a fatherly one, as we see also in 1 Thessalonians 2:10-12. He had 'begotten' them (1 Cor. 4:14-17) through the gospel he had been commissioned to preach. He saw the role of the parent as that of a giver and the child as a receiver.

Verse 15 shows that he still intends to work among them freely, presumably through the support of other churches. His self-giving would go beyond finance. Here again we see a parallel with 1 Thessalonians (1 Thess. 2:8, 9). It is often easier to reach into our pockets or purses or to write a cheque than to give costly personal service. This self-giving is well illustrated in Paul's address to the Ephesian elders at Miletus, where we see how deep and how far-ranging had been the work he had done among them when he was at Ephesus (Acts 20:17-38).

Parents may not expect much in the way of presents or gifts from their young children, but they do anticipate that love given

---

1. See Introduction, pp. 11-13 and p. 25.

will find a response in love returned. Paul finds it so very difficult to understand why it is that his own self-giving expression
of love has not been reciprocated by all the members of the
church. If he comes again and gives himself to them still more,
will they reciprocate?

Verse 16 puts it virtually beyond doubt that Paul had been
the object of calumny at Corinth and that there had been charges
of under-handedness in terms of finance. Perhaps some were
saying that the collection of money for the poor Christians in
Jerusalem would never get to its intended recipients but that it
would go straight into his pocket, and that Titus and another
Christian brother who had come to Corinth had been sent by
Paul so that this financial chicanery could be covert rather than
overt.

His comment in this verse is clearly ironic, with a touch of
facetiousness, and yet with a very serious purpose, as we see in
verses 17 and 18, where he writes very frankly. The visits made
by Titus, this other brother and Paul himself had given no cause
whatever for such allegations. Everything they had done had
been completely above board and without financial strings attached.

We see from these verses that Paul had confidence that his
financial integrity would be completely vindicated if only the
Corinthians would actually look at the facts. It is often when
rumour and innuendo triumph over actual facts that problems
come within a local church.

2. His concern for their holiness (12:19-13:4)

The question which opens verse 19 may seem strange to the
reader, for it certainly seems that Paul has been engaging in a
lengthy self-defence, and that its purpose was to get the Corinthians to think better of him. He probably recognized that the
Corinthians too might well misunderstand him in this way.

In fact, he had been motivated by concern for their spiritual well-being, and his use of the first person plural shows that Timothy (1:1) was fully with him in this. The motive has not been self-vindication but their own upbuilding. He had to establish with them the authenticity of his ministry, for otherwise he would not have been able to continue to exercise it among them, and this would certainly have been detrimental to them, for he was God's messenger to them.

He reminds them that this letter to them from himself and Timothy had come from Christians. Self-vindication was hardly an appropriate exercise for Christians to indulge in, but taking measures to secure the continuance of ministry was. He says too that this had been done 'in the sight of God', so that he was aware that God saw into his heart and was able to discern his motives.

The words, 'dear friends', are a spontaneous expression of affection for those for whom Paul wants to do nothing but good. We should remember this as we read the strong words he penned in the two following verses.

Paul had already postponed his third visit to Corinth because he wanted to give the church there time to put right the matters that were causing him concern, and he shows clearly that he still has fears about the situation there. This is one of the passages that have led some scholars to conclude that chapters 10 to 13 are from an earlier letter, sent prior to the main bulk of 2 Corinthians. See the Introduction[2] for comment on this.

Paul has written of his parental relationship with them (v. 14), but there are times when encounters between parents and children are not very pleasant for either of them (v. 20). A parent has sometimes to show love by acting strongly in discipline.

The ugly picture given in verse 20b, in which the apostle specifies his concerns for the church at Corinth, is certainly not

2. See Introduction, pp. 18-21.

the kind of idealistic image we sometimes mistakenly have of the New Testament churches. It is important to remember that the members of these churches were not perfected saints but often quite immature Christians. Just as young children often display their immaturity by squabbling, so may immature Christians – and immaturity in Christians is not always related to their age as believers (cf. Heb. 5:12)!

The faults to which he refers in verse 20 are almost all in the realm of attitudes and of utterances that express such attitudes. How significant that Paul's first concern in writing them his First Epistle was with their party-spirit (1 Cor. 1-4)! There he showed his deep concern that they should be one.

Clearly he is afraid that that spirit had not left the church. We should not however assume that everything Paul writes here is necessarily related to the party-spirit, for much could simply be indications that many of them had not really grown up as Christians and so were manifesting childishness in their relationships.

In verse 21, he expresses concern at a somewhat different level. He knows the deeply immoral environment in which the church was called to live at Corinth and the kind of things that many of the Christians will have indulged in before Christ laid hold on them (cf. 1 Cor. 6:9-11). As we see in the First Epistle (1 Cor. 5), the church had been showing little concern about at least one situation which Paul regarded as unacceptable.

In referring to 'many who had sinned earlier', is he thinking of the case of sexual immorality he addressed in 1 Corinthians 5? His words here seem too far-reaching simply to apply to that. He may well have encountered further evidence of immorality during his second visit.

Why does Paul repeat the fact that this is to be his third visit (13:1; cf. 12:14)? Some have thought that this is directly connected with his reference to 'two or three witnesses', which is a quotation from Deuteronomy 19:15, in Israel's God-given legal code. Perhaps he is saying that his three visits to them have been like the three witnesses the law required against an offender, and that they are therefore being given adequate warning.

Alternatively, he may simply be saying that this important principle in the Law must also apply in church discipline. Certainly the need for adequate witnesses of wrong-doing is a matter of simple justice.

It is not impossible, of course, that both interpretations are correct, and he is saying not only that the old principle needs to be properly applied but also that, as an extension of that principle, he has given them adequate warning by his two, soon to be three, visits. Adequate warning is nearly as important a principle as adequate witness. He may also have viewed this as comparable to the threefold approach to issues of discipline which our Lord enjoined in Matthew 18:15-18.

Verse 2a may have a hidden as well as an obvious purpose, for Paul here shows that he was not one thing in person and another in his letters (cf. 10:10, 11).

On his return there would be decisive discipline. Paul knew full well that a church that is without discipline cannot have a clear witness in the community in which God has placed it.

There had apparently been a demand at Corinth that he should provide proof that he was a mouthpiece of Christ, proof of his genuine apostleship. This was, of course, the reason for his defence, his 'boasting' and 'foolishness' in recent chapters.

In contrast to the false apostles (cf. 11:19, 20), he much preferred the gentle approach, but if discipline was to be needed, Christ would show his power through him when Paul paid them his next visit. This was because, although he was crucified in weakness, he was now alive with all power.

What then does he mean by the words, 'he was crucified in

weakness' (v. 4)? This surely refers to the fact that Christ assumed human nature in all its weakness (compare the similar concept of 'poverty' in 8:9, and the comment there), that he did not resist when they came to fetch him from the Garden of Gethsemane, and that he allowed himself to be impaled on the tree instead of calling for legions of angels to protect him (Matt. 26:53) or using his own miraculous powers.

After the cross came the resurrection, which was accomplished by God's power in vindication of Jesus, as the early preachers never tired of declaring (e.g. in Acts 2:23, 24; 10:39; 17:31). This means that he is alive now and with all power at his disposal. So Christ was well able to deal in discipline with the situation at Corinth, and to do it through Paul as his apostolic agent.

For Paul too, because of his union with Christ, shares both in the weakness and the power of Christ (cf. Gal. 2:20 and Rom. 6). As a consequence of this, there are two sides to his ministry. He is called to share, on the one hand, both the meekness and willingness to suffer which Christ showed and, on the other, the power and authority which he now exercises.

3. His call for their self-examination (13:5-10)

The Corinthians have been subjecting Paul and his claim to apostleship to intense scrutiny. Perhaps, he suggests, it is time for them to turn that scrutiny on themselves.

Are they Christians? It is a strange fact of the New Testament epistles that this appears to be the only passage where such a question is asked of the readers. This probably indicates that at that time, because of the cost in terms of ostracism or even persecution, few would profess conversion who had not come to a true faith, although obviously this was not invariable, as a passage like 1 John 2:18,19 shows.

Even here, what Paul says is probably not intended to raise

real doubts about their conversion, but is rather to be seen in the context of his sparring with the Corinthians over the questions they were asking about him. It is true, of course, that his words do allow for the possibility of the failure of some of them to pass the test.

He does not say what tests they were to apply, although a study of the First Epistle of John will indicate the kind of tests of real faith and genuine spiritual life which are appropriate in every age of the church.

It is somewhat ironic that discovering that their own faith was true would in fact point in the direction of the genuineness of Paul's apostleship (v. 6). Why? Because it was through him that they had come to faith in Christ in the first place, so that this said something about God's use of him in this way.

In verse 7, Paul shows again that his chief desire was not for self-vindication (see the comment on 12:18). He prayed that they might make progress in the right way, and he was more concerned about this than that he should himself be vindicated. In Romans 9:3, he expressed an even stronger desire for the well-being of others and at the deepest cost to himself.

Verse 8 serves to underline this. Paul is more than content simply to allow the truth to be exposed to view, for what is true must triumph in the end.

Verse 9 should be read in the light of verses 2 to 4. The weakness of which Paul writes here is in fact the gentleness and meekness of Christ (10:1), which he so much wanted to show to the Corinthians. He would be able to demonstrate this to them if he discovered on his arrival that they were in fact strong in the Lord and if they were moving towards that perfection at which it is proper for Christians to aim (Phil. 3:12-14).

Verse 10 is as near to a statement of the general purpose of this epistle as we can find, and it is equally suitable whether chapters 10 to 13 constitute a separate letter from the rest of 2

Corinthians or are an integral part of it.[3]

He is so keen to be able to come in a spirit of gentleness and not of strong discipline. He saw the main purpose of Christ's commission to be to edify them, not to subject them to strong discipline.

The language here may be intentionally reminiscent of Jeremiah 1:10, where the prophet is told that God has appointed him 'over nations and kingdoms to uproot and tear down, to destroy and overthrow, to build and to plant.'

Jeremiah's situation and Paul's were very different, for the prophet was commissioned to call to repentance a nation bent on a course which could lead only to its self-destruction, while Paul's God-given task was to edify a group of people who had already been brought to repentance and faith in Christ. Even so, there may be a veiled allusion to a possible comparison, which would certainly hold if in fact Paul had to come to exercise strong discipline.

Some questions for personal reflection:

1. How much do I give of myself to those to whom God has called me to minister for him?

2. 'Everything we do, dear friends, is for your strengthening.' Can I apply these words to my attitude to any who are influenced by my Christian work?

3. Is there still a place today for church discipline?

---

3. See Introduction, pp. 18-21.

21: A WONDERFUL CONCLUSION (13:11-14)

Literary endings are often not as well known as literary beginnings.

There was a time when every schoolgirl recognized, '"Christmas won't be Christmas without any presents," grumbled Jo', as the opening words of *Little Women*, but who could say what its final sentence was? This used to be true also among Christians in relation to *Pilgrim's Progress*, which begins, 'As I walked through the wilderness of this world....'

This applies even to some Bible books. Everybody knows how Genesis begins, but how does it end? If you look it up you will notice what a contrast there is between the start and the finish.

In Scripture however there is a factor that makes the ending of some Bible books most memorable, for each of the Gospels closes with the story of the resurrection of Christ and what followed this. Happy endings used to be standard in a certain type of fictional literature, so standard in fact that they ceased to be memorable just because they were not distinctive, but the truth of God's great act of raising Christ from the dead was unique and unforgettable.

The last verse of Second Corinthians is extremely well-known but for a different reason. It would be very difficult to find a Christian who does not know it, even if he or she is unaware of its location in Scripture, for it is used with great frequency in Christian services, often twice a Sunday. In fact, it is almost certainly the most-quoted verse in the whole Bible.

It is however only part of Paul's conclusion and so we must look also at the verses which precede it.

1. Exhortations (13:11)

In many civilisations, not least in the Near East, salutations on meeting and leaving people tended, and in some places still tend, to be lengthy and determined in their form by elaborate rules of etiquette and protocol. Everything Paul says in greeting and taking his leave of others, however, is coloured by his Christian faith. There may be some employment of standard formalities, but they are always adapted to serve spiritual ends. See the comments on 1:1, 2.

His word of farewell here, (translated as 'goodbye') is a single one, and this is the only place in the New Testament where the word is used in this sense.

It has in it something of the cheerfulness of the French, *au revoir!*, or of the German *auf wieder sehen!* or of the English 'See you again!' or the West of Scotland, 'Goodbye for now!' It is said that all these had their origins in superstition, and this may be so, but there may also be in all of them some suggestion of pleasure at the thought of a further meeting.

Paul's word is one with a cheerful ring about it, and it was actually used more often when meeting people than when leaving them. As a word of farewell, its meaning and mood could almost be conveyed by our colloquial word, 'Cheerio!' He hopes, of course, that conditions at Corinth will now make it a pleasure to be with the Christians there (7:8-13).

He adds warmth to this word, by addressing his readers as 'brothers'. He is an apostle, and out of necessity he has been at pains to underscore the authenticity of this office, but he is also their brother.

The word translated 'Aim for perfection,' means 'put in order' and is often used in the sense of 'restore' or 'mend'. This was most appropriate in view of the problems of which Paul was aware at the church.

The verb translated 'listen to my appeal' can also mean 'be

of good comfort' and it would be apt here in either of these meanings. The first underlines the word that precedes it, and the second would remind the readers of the first chapter, where Paul writes of the comfort Christians may receive in suffering and with which they can comfort others (1:3-11).

The remainder of verse 11 clearly relates to their tendencies to division. These were very evident to Paul when he wrote them his First Epistle, and he regarded them as so serious that he began that letter by addressing the issue, spending four chapters on it.

'The God of love and peace will be with you,' is a reminder not only of God's concern for their unity, but of the fact that he is also the source of it and that love is indispensable to it. Paul has already extolled God-given love in 1 Corinthians 13.

2. Greetings (13:12, 13)

The kiss is an expression of love and is much used in the Near East as well as in many other places as a form of salutation as well, but, of course, with implications of good relationships.

Paul refers to it here as 'a holy kiss', as he does also in Romans 16:16, 1 Corinthians 16:20 and 1 Thessalonians 5:26. Clearly this too had been transformed by Christians from a fairly formal sign of greeting to an expression of the love of God, of which Paul writes in the previous verse. Just as in its use at the close of 1 Corinthians, he may be implying here that it should be a sign among them of a love transcending their differences of outlook.

Paul writes from Macedonia[1] and, just as he has used the Macedonians as an encouragement to the Corinthians to give generously for the relief of the poor (8:1-7), so he now conveys their greetings. In this way he was able to express the oneness of the wider church with the Corinthians in the love of Christ.

---

1. See 'Chronology of Paul's Contacts with the Church at Corinth' on p. 25.

3. Benediction (13:14)

This well-known verse is Trinitarian in form. Quite rightly, we speak of the Divine Trinity as Father, Son and Holy Spirit, and we attach some significance to the order. It is however noteworthy that this, although the most frequent order in the New Testament, is not invariable, and we see from a passage like this that other orders are quite appropriate. This is because the three Persons are equal in nature and so in honour.

The order here seems to be that of Christian experience. Paul has written movingly in 8:9 of the grace of Christ, and we can see that for him this grace found its great expression in his atoning death (5:14-6:2). It is here at the cross that our saving experience of God finds its beginning.

Through the death of Christ we are introduced to the love of God, for his death was the supreme demonstration of God's love (Rom. 5:8) and, at the same time, of course, of the love of Christ (Gal. 2:20; Eph. 5:1, 25).

We might perhaps expect either 'the Father' or 'God the Father' instead of simply 'God'. In fact, the New Testament writers often refer to the Father simply as God. The reason for this is that, in the Old Testament, prior to the express revelation of the Trinitarian nature of God, the Son was presented mostly in terms of Messianic prophecy, in which the Christ was to come in fulfilment of the promise of God, and the Spirit is viewed as the Agent of God, active among his people. It is natural therefore that, although the fully Divine nature of the Son and the Spirit is abundantly clear in the New Testament, the term 'God' should continue to be used mostly of the One whom Christ taught his disciples to call 'Father'.

What does 'the fellowship of the Holy Spirit' mean? Some have interpreted it as the fellowship the Christian has with the Holy Spirit, but this seems unlikely. If the grace and love here are those that emanate from the Son and the Father respectively, then it seems most likely that Paul is thinking here of the fellowship which has the Spirit as its Divine Source.

If that is so, then it coheres well with verse 11, for peace among the saints is expressed in their fellowship, created among them by the Spirit whose work not only binds them to Christ but also constitutes them together as his body (1 Cor. 12:12, 13).

Here then, at the close of his epistle, Paul shows that concern for the unity of the church at Corinth which has clearly been in his heart throughout his correspondence with them, most explicitly in the First Epistle, but also in the Second. Such loving unity in Christ is not of human creation, but comes from God through his Spirit.

We should treasure it.

Some questions for personal reflection:

1. If I use the last verse of 2 Corinthians in services of worship or in public prayer, is it so formal as to lose its meaning for me – and even for others?

2. What are the main lessons I have learned for my own Christian service from studying this great epistle?

Other titles by Geoffrey Grogan,
published by Christian Focus

Wrestling With The Big Issues

In this much appreciated book, Geoffrey Grogan examines the principles and methods used by Paul to assess and solve the doctrinal and practical problems that appeared in the early Christian Church. Most of these problems have reappeared throughout church history, and can be found today in evangelical churches. Geoffrey Grogan is convinced that the answers to many of today's difficulties are to be found in applying to current situations the Spirit-inspired instructions of the apostle.

Howard Marshall says about *Wrestling With The Big Issues*: 'This book is remarkable for being written by a New Testament scholar in such a simple and relevant way that any reader will be able to understand what is being said and see how Paul's letters still speak to Christians today.'

Sinclair Ferguson comments that 'Geoffrey Grogan brings to his teaching, preaching and writing a life-time of study. He combines careful exposition with practical care.'

And Clive Calver says that 'Geoffrey Grogan possesses the uncanny knack of setting truth on fire: here the personality of the apostle shines through its pages; the life of a man who Christ used to transform the history of his church.'

ISBN 1 85792 051 1   256 Pages

In the Focus on the Bible commentary series, Geoffrey Grogan has also contributed the commentary on Mark.